Inclusive Research

Bloomsbury Research Methods

Edited by Graham Crow and Mark Elliot

The Bloomsbury Research Methods series provides authoritative introductions to a range of research methods which are at the forefront of developments in a range of disciplines.

Each volume sets out the key elements of the particular method and features examples of its application, drawing on a consistent structure across the whole series. Written in an accessible style by leading experts in the field, this series is an innovative pedagogical and research resource.

Also available in the series

Community Studies, Graham Crow
Diary Method, Ruth Bartlett and Christine Milligan
GIS, Nick Bearman
Qualitative Longitudinal Research, Bren Neale
Quantitative Longitudinal Data Analysis, Vernon Gayle and Paul Lambert
Rhythmanalysis, Dawn Lyon

Forthcoming in the series

Embodied Inquiry, Jennifer Leigh and Nicole Brown
Statistical Modelling in R, Kevin Ralston, Vernon Gayle, Roxanne Connelly and Chris Playford

Inclusive
Research

Research Methods

Melanie Nind

BLOOMSBURY ACADEMIC
LONDON • NEW YORK • OXFORD • NEW DELHI • SYDNEY

BLOOMSBURY ACADEMIC
Bloomsbury Publishing Plc
50 Bedford Square, London, WC1B 3DP, UK
1385 Broadway, New York, NY 10018, USA

BLOOMSBURY, BLOOMSBURY ACADEMIC and the Diana logo are trademarks of Bloomsbury
Publishing Plc

First published Open Access under a Creative Commons license in 2014
as *What is Inclusive Research?*, this title is now also available as part
of the Bloomsbury Research Methods series.
This edition published 2021

Series design by Charlotte James
Cover image © shuoshu / iStock

A catalogue record for this book is available from the British Library.

Library of Congress Cataloging-in-Publication Data
Names: Nind, Melanie, author.
Title: What is inclusive research / Melanie Nind.
Other titles: Inclusive research
Description: London ; New York : Bloomsbury Academic, [2020] | Series: "What is?" research
methods series, 2048-6812 | Includes bibliographical references and index.
Identifiers: LCCN 2020034770 (print) | LCCN 2020034771 (ebook) | ISBN 9781350188778
(hardback) | ISBN 9781350188761 (paperback) | ISBN 9781350188792 (epub) |
ISBN 9781350188808 (ebook)
Subjects: LCSH: Social sciences–Research–Methodology. | Research–Social aspects.
Classification: LCC H62 .N663 2020 (print) | LCC H62 (ebook) | DDC 001.4/2–dc23
LC record available at https://lccn.loc.gov/2020034770
LC ebook record available at https://lccn.loc.gov/2020034771

ISBN: HB: 978-1-3501-8877-8
PB: 978-1-3501-8876-1
ePDF: 978-1-3501-8880-8
eBook: 978-1-3501-8879-2

Series: Bloomsbury Research Methods

Typeset by Deanta Global Publishing Services, Chennai, India

To find out more about our authors and books visit www.bloomsbury.com
and sign up for our newsletters.

Contents

Series foreword

The idea behind this book series is a simple one: to provide concise and accessible introductions to frequently used research methods and of current issues in research methodology. Books in the series have been written by experts in their fields with a brief to write about their subject for a broad audience.

The series has been developed through a partnership between Bloomsbury and the UK's National Centre for Research Methods (NCRM). The original 'What is?' Research Methods Series sprang from the eponymous strand at NCRM's Research Methods Festivals.

This relaunched series reflects changes in the research landscape, embracing research methods innovation and interdisciplinarity. Methodological innovation is the order of the day, while still maintaining an emphasis on accessibility to a wide audience. The format allows researchers who are new to a field to gain an insight into its key features, while also providing a useful update on recent developments for people who have had some prior acquaintance with it. All readers should find it helpful to be taken through the discussion of key terms, the history of how the method or methodological issue has developed, and the assessment of the strengths and possible weaknesses of the approach through analysis of illustrative examples.

This book is devoted to inclusive research, which is an area of research methods that is witnessing dramatic changes as the relationships between people involved in the research process are rethought and reconfigured. Dissatisfaction with their treatment as research 'subjects' by 'experts' has prompted various groups of people to challenge the idea that they are there to have research done 'on' them, and to mount a sustained campaign to be treated more inclusively in the research process. Many others who have been trained as researchers have been sympathetic to this push for greater inclusion at all stages of the production and dissemination of knowledge, and the result has been a move towards less rigid hierarchies in relationships and a greater sense of shared purpose. In the course of these changes, the language of research practice has also altered, with new understandings of what constitutes 'research' and who qualifies as a 'researcher'. These changes have been referred to as examples of the more general process of the democratization of research and, as that term implies, this process has its political aspects, including tensions and negotiations about the power to set agendas and standards. Melanie Nind's book takes readers through the recent history and current state of these debates about what is involved in inclusive research, and why it is important to pursue inclusivity as a goal even though its achievement is not always straightforward. As is the case in other areas of methodological innovation, changing practice around inclusivity has required experimentation and a preparedness to take risks and to venture into new territories, leaving behind the safe familiarity of established practices. The fruit of these endeavours has been to allow the voices of people previously excluded from research to have their say, and in the process to pose fundamental questions more generally about why, for whom and by whom research is undertaken.

The books cannot provide information about their subject matter down to a fine level of detail, but they will equip readers with a powerful sense of reasons why it deserves to be taken seriously and, it is hoped, with the enthusiasm to put that knowledge into practice.

Tables and figures

Tables

Figures

Acknowledgements

I am grateful to colleagues who provided feedback on the first draft of this book: Anne Collis, Graham Crow, Gina Sherwood and Hilra Vinha.

I also acknowledge all the contributors to the ESRC-funded 'Doing Research Inclusively, Doing Research Well?' study, from whom I learned a great deal; reflection on that learning has helped me to shape this book.

1 Inclusive research defined

Introduction

This book introduces readers to inclusive research including how to recognize it, understand it, conduct it and know when it is done well. I have
a developing – rather than fully developed – stance on inclusive research
myself. As I discuss further in Chapter 5, I have adopted a more inclusive
approach at some times than at others and I have recently engaged in a
study of what quality means in inclusive research. The quality study (Nind
and Vinha, 2012) involved focus group dialogue with over 60 inclusive
researchers/supporters and funders of inclusive research to co-create
knowledge about this way of approaching research and supporting social
inclusion. I am convinced by the argument (e.g. Walmsley and Johnson,
2003) that inclusive research requires critical scrutiny and I engage in this
throughout the book.

Inclusive research encompasses a range of approaches and methods and
these may be variously referred to in the literature as participatory, emancipatory, partnership and user-led research – even peer research, community research, activist scholarship, decolonizing or indigenous research – the
list goes on. By way of illustration, the International Collaboration for
Participatory Health Research (ICPHR, 2013) add to the list of research
traditions in this camp: Participatory Rural Appraisal (PRA), Liberationist
Research approaches, Action Research, Human/Cooperative/Appreciative
Inquiry, Community-Based Participatory Research (CBPR), Constructivist
Research, Feminist Research, Empowerment Evaluation and Democratic
Dialogue. Many of these terms are in more frequent usage than the term
'inclusive research' that I have opted to use for this book. I use inclusive
research deliberately as the most generic term, however, to embrace this
whole family of approaches, all of which reflect a particular turn towards
democratization of the research process.

It is worth noting at this juncture that alongside common threads and
distinctive features among research approaches that might be considered

inclusive, there is variation in terms and meanings that relate to international variations. I write from the United Kingdom where inclusive research is emerging as a term. It is used differently here from action research where the ideas of Kurt Lewin, Lawrence Stenhouse and John Elliott have been influential in a concept evolving to stress the personal, professional and political in educational action research in particular (Noffke, 2009). In the United States, collaborative research is a similar umbrella term, more commonly used to embrace research that actively engages communities and policy makers in conducting research, including framing the research problem and interpreting and acting on the findings. Minkler and Wallerstein (2008) regard CBPR also as an 'overarching' term: for action research, participatory action research (PAR), mutual inquiry and feminist action research, all of which stem from a reaction to a dominant research tradition and bring a new 'orientation' based on mutual respect and co-learning. They note the difference between the way that action research is understood in the United Kingdom and Australia compared to the United States, and the different geographical roots of PAR in work with oppressed peoples in Asia, Africa and Latin America. Wallerstein and Duran (2008) similarly note Northern and Southern traditions and variations. The Durham Community Research Team (2011) observes that while the concept of CBPR is most used in US health research it is used in the United Kingdom also.

In this first chapter some of these nuances are acknowledged and some, by necessity, are set aside as inclusive, collaborative, participatory, emancipatory, participatory action, and partnership/user-led/child-led research are defined and explained in relation to each other and to the fields and arguments from which they have evolved. Within each of the research approaches defined in this chapter there are elements of consensus, elements where there are differences of emphasis, and matters of greater contention. This includes discussion of the ways in which they overlap and what makes them distinctive. In later chapters the rationale for inclusive research in different fields and disciplines is explained (Chapter 2), different models of inclusive research are presented through illustrative examples (Chapter 3), the challenges and criticisms – together with responses to these – are discussed (Chapter 4), and the quality, status and future of inclusive research is explored (Chapter 5).

Inclusive research is a growing field and one in which researchers can be passionate, often arguing that inclusive research (or their particular variety of it) is superior in some way. Contested matters include who gets to participate in research (Cornwall and Jewkes, 1995; Holland et al., 2008), what constitutes active participation (Gallacher and Gallagher, 2008), whether it is the quality of the participation or the quality of the research that matters more (Freeman and Mathison, 2009; Greene, 2009), whether inclusive or participatory research is necessarily 'ethically or morally superior' or 'more enabling' (Holland et al., 2008; Frankham, 2009) and whether participation and emancipation can be decoupled (Danieli and Woodhams, 2005). There are also debates about the individuals, groups and topics for whom inclusive research is helpful or necessary, and about what is driving the push to make the research inclusive. To enter such debates it is first necessary to look at the various ways in which these kinds of research are conceptualized.

Defining inclusive research

The term inclusive research can be found prominently in the field of learning disability[1] research and in the work of Walmsley and Johnson (2003). They use the term to embrace 'a range of research approaches that traditionally have been termed "participatory", "action" or "emancipatory"' (p. 10). Importantly, they pinpoint the commonality between these: 'Such research involves people who may otherwise be seen as subjects for the research as instigators of ideas, research designers, interviewers, data analysts, authors, disseminators and users' (p. 10). In answer to why yet another term is needed for this kind of research, Walmsley and Johnson are clear: inclusive research as a term allows for the blurred and shifting boundaries between, for example, feminist, participatory and emancipatory research and it 'has the advantage of being less cumbersome and more readily explained to people unfamiliar with the nuances of academic debate' (p. 10). It is a term that can be used across fields and disciplines.

Inclusive research can be usefully thought of as research that changes the dynamic between research/researchers and the people who are usually researched: it is conceived as research *with*, *by* or sometimes *for* them (see Griffiths, 1998), and in contrast to research *on* them. Inclusive

---

[1] In this book, the term learning disability (and people with learning disabilities) is used to refer to people with intellectual impairment; this is interchangeable with learning difficulties in the United Kingdom, but not in the United States.

research shares common ground with qualitative research more widely, particularly the concern with grounding research in the experiences and views of respondents (Kiernan, 1999). Most qualitative research, though, retains the status quo of the researcher being the person who defines the questions, handles and controls the interpretation of the data, and makes and communicates the conclusions; it is this that is unsettled in inclusive research. Kiernan (1999) regarded such a turn as a new paradigm but with variations in how it was understood and enacted by traditional and new 'co-researchers'. Fenge (2010) in the title of her paper about PAR with older lesbians and gay men, 'Striving towards Inclusive Research', reminds us that journeying towards being inclusive is at the heart of what the shift in paradigm is about.

Predictably, inclusive research cannot be translated into one particular way of doing things; the options or permutations for this are extensive (Walmsley, 2004). Nonetheless, it is possible to pinpoint the characteristics and principles underpinning inclusive research. Walmsley and Johnson (2003, p. 64) do this in relation to people with learning disabilities:

- The research problem must be one that is owned (not necessarily initiated) by disabled people.
- It should further the interests of disabled people; non-disabled researchers should be on the side of people with learning disabilities.
- It should be collaborative – people with learning disabilities should be involved in the process of doing the research.
- People with learning disabilities should be able to exert some control over process and outcomes.
- The research question, process and reports must be accessible to people with learning disabilities.

An alternative umbrella term to inclusive research might be CBPR, as discussed earlier, or collaborative research, as used for example by the University of California Center for Collaborative Research for an Equitable California (CCREC). They describe collaborative research as 'engaged scholarship in action, in which university researchers, community members, and policy makers respect the knowledge that each partner brings to the discussion so that together they might know better how to understand the complex problems facing our communities and how to design and implement research-based responses to those problems' (CCREC, n.d.). They also recognize the plethora of similar labels attached to such research, including community-based research, CBPR, engaged scholarship and PAR. The overlap with inclusive research is clear to see. While throughout this book I use inclusive research as my umbrella term, I acknowledge that collaborative research as a term might work equally well if it were not also used to refer to all kinds of collaborations, for example, between parties of equal status or between universities and business partners, which reflect a completely different agenda. Similarly action research terms are problematic in that not all action research has a participatory element and CBPR carries with it the concept of community that does not travel well across cultures and languages (Springett et al., 2011). While the nature of this book series and book theme necessitates using an overarching term, I also, at times, adapt choice of language to reflect political and other contexts as Springett et al. (2011) argue is necessary.

Defining participatory research

To see how the term inclusive research also allows for the overlap and reciprocity between participatory and emancipatory research these too need to be defined. Cancian (1989) sees participatory research as involving democratic relationships to produce knowledge which incorporates participants' everyday knowledge, and to solve problems. Bourke (2009, p. 458) offers a definition of participatory research as 'a research process which involves those being researched in the decision-making and conduct of the research, including project planning, research design, data collection and analysis, and/or the distribution and application of research findings'. This definition indicates that it is the people being researched who are participating and that the participation is comprehensively across the multiple stages of the research. It stresses involvement in the process of doing the research rather merely providing data for it, which is echoed by many. As with inclusive research, many writing specifically about participatory research tend to resist further delineation of what this involves in practice.

Byrne et al. (2009, pp. 67–8) address the inherent motivation for participatory research: 'participatory researchers seek to engage in meaningful partnerships with the researched seeking meaningful data for social transformation.' Thus, participatory research has an element of doing things in a more participatory way for a reason – to bring about change (Durham Community Research Team, 2011; ICPHR, 2013). At this point there are different emphases among the various advocates of this kind of research. The change might be about how knowledge is produced, including 'a de-privileging of "researcher-only" expertise' (Byrne et al., 2009, p. 68; ICPHR, 2013), or about what the knowledge is used for. For Fenge (2010, p. 880) this is about 'lay researchers ... setting the agenda for the research to be undertaken', and for Browne et al. (2012) it is about influencing the agendas of those with power while empowering those without. The social change associated with participatory research is partly achieved by making research more of a dialogue; a crucial element is academic and lay researchers[2] working closely together to benefit from each other's perspectives.

In participatory research the contention is mostly about whether participatory research is a set of techniques or a political philosophy (Cleaver, 1999). Methods can be important. Dyslexic doctoral researcher Spires has explained to me the importance of her video methods in doing research with university students with dyslexia: providing alternatives to producing and reading written text, for all their benefit. Similarly, Ayrton (2012) sought fitting methods for her research with mothers in Southern Sudan where literacy is limited. By stringing beads on to a leather thong to make bracelets, she supported the women to tell their life stories without employing artefacts associated with education and literacy. This also provided them with a valued product of the reflections. Nonetheless, many would argue that methods are not the essence of participatory research.

ICPHR (2013) stress that participatory research, or participatory health research which is their particular concern, is a research paradigm rather than a research method. This means that it is the underlying assumptions that matter most, or as Cook (2012) argues, such research 'inhabits different spaces and offers different ways of seeing'. Fals-Borda and Rahman (1991) even refer to participatory research approaches as a range of epistemological principles or paradigms. Cooke and Kothari (2001), Punch (2002), Kesby (2007) and Clark (2010) have all argued for participatory design rather than for participatory methods. Participatory methods for research with children are often devised and referred to as child friendly, but Todd (2012, p. 193) explains that 'the adoption of methods as seemingly

---

[2] I use the term lay researcher, adopted by INVOLVE, as it offers a distinction from professional researchers and can be inclusive of people of any age or identity (see Ross et al., 2005).

more "child friendly" misses the complexities of the research situation, as a contested and constructed site.' Thomson (2007, p. 209) is also explicit about this, arguing that 'participation is not inherent to the research methods themselves as some accounts of participatory methods seem to imply.' She has an alternative concept of participatory research as 'spatial practice'. Spaces for life experiences to be discussed may be 'closed' (or 'invited') spaces, directed by the researcher, or 'claimed/created space', in which participants can create new power and possibilities. Cornwall and Jewkes (1995, p. 667) similarly argue that 'what is distinctive about participatory research is not the methods, but the methodological contexts of their application' – the researchers' attitudes on the various research problems leading them to adapt ordinary methods for use by and with ordinary people. Also contentious, they argue, is whether participatory research is 'a universal panacea for the problems besetting conventional practice' or 'biased, impressionistic and unreliable'. This panacea question is discussed further in Chapter 4.

Defining emancipatory research

Emancipatory research is usually defined in more overtly political terms than participatory research. It 'has been widely taken to mean only that sort of research which is controlled by those who are implicated by it, with the aim of the empowerment of those participants through the research process and outcomes' (Frankham, 2009, p. 3, after Barnes, 2003). Oliver (1992, p. 110), a major proponent of emancipatory research for disabled people, describes it as being about confronting social oppression. This for him necessitates a fundamental change in 'the social relations of research production' such that researchers have to 'learn how to put their knowledge and skills at the disposal of their research subjects, for them to use in whatever ways they choose' (p. 111). Oliver's criteria for emancipatory research include the following: it is disabled people who gain; the research combats social oppression; disabled people are in control of the resources (otherwise it is more like participatory research); and the research process is politicized. Disabled people's groups offer guidance on this, thereby making clear, and in some ways policing, what is seen as acceptable. For Oliver, emancipatory research is the ideal and participatory or action research is what people settle for when this cannot be achieved; moreover, settling for less involves a 'limited vision of the possible' (1997, p. 26) and a reinforcement of the status quo in terms of power. A useful metaphor he uses to help make the distinction is that participatory/action research approaches 'allow previously excluded groups to be included in the (research) game as it is, whereas emancipatory strategies are concerned about both conceptualising and creating a different game, where no one is excluded in the first place' (p. 26).

Oliver is not alone in attempting to distinguish emancipatory research from other forms. Zarb (1992) similarly emphasizes the requirement for change in the social and material relations of research production. Chappell (2000) argues that the distinction between participatory and emancipatory research is that the latter is accountable to disabled people and their organizations. Walmsley (2004, p. 66) distinguishes them by noting that, in participatory research, non-disabled people have an enduring role in a way that is not true of emancipatory research. McLarty and Gibson (2000, p. 138), referring to emancipatory research by practitioners rather than disabled people, stress their ownership of the research problem. They draw on Heron (1996, p. 28) to delineate two levels of empowerment, one involving productive use of 'informants' and one 'when informants are empowered by being initiated in, and by collaborating in, the research design itself and the values embodied in it'. Thus the empowerment is important alongside the ownership. Similarly, coming back to disabled people again, French and Swain (1997) combine these two core features. They note the insistence within emancipatory research 'that disabled people should be in control (rather than merely participate in) the entire research process' (p. 27). They define it also as 'a form of education and political action', 'towards the achievement of their liberation' (p. 28). Some people take the position that research about disabled people should be done only by disabled people, and so on. Emancipatory researchers, therefore, may also be regarded as activists (Kiernan, 1999), and as change agents to a far greater extent than participatory researchers.

Defining participatory action research

Participatory research and emancipatory research clearly have common and distinct features, but these are muddied somewhat in another member of the family of inclusive research approaches – PAR. This is a form of action research that has been written about extensively and therefore I do not dwell on it in this book. Rather I refer you to the PAR toolkit from

Pain et al. (n.d.) and to Fals-Borda's (1991) ingredients of PAR: education, research and socio-political action, bringing different agents to work together for social transformation. Nonetheless, it is noteworthy that research in which ordinary people participate or take control is often conceptualized as PAR. We might think of this as a cousin of participatory or emancipatory research, sharing a 'commitment to break away from traditional research conventions by involving the "researched" in some or all stages of the research process (Pain, 2004)' (Cahill, 2007, p. 298), or even as 'architects' (Torre and Fine, 2006, cited by Cahill, 2007, p. 298) of it. McTaggart (1997, p. 28) refers to their agency in producing knowledge and improving practice – their 'authentic participation'. Thus, also shared is the concern with the research making things better for the people involved and affected, while removing knowledge production from the elite (Rahman, 1991). In PAR there is perhaps greater emphasis on process and on seeing people as change agents (Cahill, 2007). PAR has emerged from grassroots (feminist, antiracist) movements and is very much a 'bottom up' approach (Cahill, 2007, p. 308). Other cousins are activist participatory research and PRA (Chambers, 1992; Narayanasamy, 2009) where the concern is with underprivileged peoples and political action with outsiders acting as facilitators or catalysts. In PRA, local people 'share, enhance and analyse their knowledge of life . . . to plan and to act' (Chambers, 1992). The key premise in PAR, though, is the notion of exchanging expertise and working together in a process in which action and research are simultaneous and inseparable.

Defining partnership, user-led or child-led research

Not everyone favours the language of participation and emancipation and for some the term 'user-led' research reflects that the crucial issue might just be who works together on, or who leads, the research. Service users are often involved in research about services when there is a desire to incorporate, first hand, their direct experience of the service (Frankham, 2009). Thus, in such 'partnership research', the particular 'way of knowing' (p. 17) of service users (or consumers, patients, pupils) is used to inform the planning and conduct of the research, empowering them along the way and generating useful, authentic knowledge. There has been significant growth in use of the partnership research where control of the research process is shared between service users and academic allies (Frankham,

2009) and also some growth in user-controlled research (Boxall et al., 2007), which most closely parallels emancipatory research.

Kellett (2005a, 2011) has done much to promote the idea of child-led research including research led by young children and specifically those in middle childhood. Here again the issue is ownership and control, but this case is different from emancipatory research. It is often adults/academic researchers who argue that children should be in the controlling seat, rather than children claiming this as their rightful position in research production of knowledge about them.

Returning to inclusive research

Returning to inclusive research as a useful term to embrace a range of related approaches it can be helpful to visualize their relationship as a Venn diagram, as shown in Figure 1.1, imagining inclusive research as encircling them all. This image is in keeping with the stance of Walmsley and Johnson (2003) and French and Swain (1997) that participatory and emancipatory research share certain characteristics, despite their different social and historical roots. While the overlap may not be great, these are at least complementary approaches to achieving meaningful social change through research. The problem – and potential – of this visual model is that it raises questions about whether it should include three equally sized

Figure 1.1 A family of overlapping approaches.

circles with equally proportioned overlaps or whether PAR is more of a subset of participatory research or of emancipatory research, and so on. The point is that people see the overlaps differently and that the conceptual boundaries between these different approaches are inevitably blurred. An alternative visual model might be that shown in Figure 1.2, which represents the idea of a continuum in which power is more shared or less shared. This is the model that Freeman and Mathison (2009) envisage when they describe a continuum of adult-led, adult-centred research through to youth-centred, youth-led research. It is also the model of participatory research described by Holland et al. (2008, p. 4) involving a range of approaches from simply inviting children and young people as participants in research, through data collected through 'child-centred' methods, to training children and young people as researchers to study their own topics and ultimately giving them control over the research process itself. The continuum proposed by Cornwall (2008) goes from (tokenistic) co-option through compliance, consultation, co-operation and co-learning to collective action. Coad and Evans (2008) similarly use the idea of a continuum of involvement in, specifically data analysis, from adults doing it and children helping to verify adults' understanding of the data, to children and young people undertaking the analysis, with a middle position of adults facilitating and working alongside children and young people. Kiernan (1999, p. 45) holds a similar position when discussing research involving people with learning disabilities, arguing that 'the difference between participatory and emancipatory paradigms may be more a matter of emphasis than kind', with participatory research a 'step toward emancipatory research' that is 'more practicable'. Kellett (2005a), in contrast, would not support the common ground suggested by this continuum model. She argues that 'research *by* children is fundamentally different from adult research *about* children and we cannot use the same norms of reference nor the

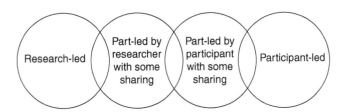

Figure 1.2 A continuum of overlapping approaches.

same terms of measurement and assessment' (p. 30). She does not present child-led research as sitting alongside child-participatory research as equal. For her (after Oliver), the pinnacle is research that is led by children, with 'every decision, every action, every word in every sentence . . . sourced, discussed and approved by the young people to ensure their own voice [is] neither diluted nor distorted' (Kellett, 2010, p. 42). For some, once 'the researched', whether child or adult, is in control of the research it becomes distinct from everything else on the continuum (see also Beresford, 2002; Frankham, 2009).

Moving on from definitions

I have defined in this chapter what I and others mean by inclusive research and related research approaches. By way of introducing the rest of the book I also need to say a little about their varied uptake and importance. In the field of disability research the debate about doing research on, with, for or by disabled people has been sufficiently prominent in sociological, geographical, health and social work arenas to mean that the question of participation of disabled people would almost always be asked. The opposite is the case in the field of psychology, where participatory research would still often be seen as radically new. The depth as well as breadth of reach is patchy. People with learning disabilities have moved from being objects of research to becoming interviewers involved in service evaluation, self-advocates having established their desire and ability to be involved in planning and conducting research, disseminating it, even commissioning and reviewing it (*British Journal of Learning Disabilities*, 2012 special issue; Nind and Vinha, 2012). The trend towards participatory and emancipatory research has been evident in some studies of poverty, in gender studies and in aspects of educational research (Frankham, 2009). In the field of children and young people there has been increased involvement, especially of older children/teenagers as co-researchers. Techniques seeking children's engagement in research have 'generated widespread interdisciplinary and global interest' (Coad and Evans, 2008, p. 41). In children's geography and childhood studies a participatory approach is 'almost universally lauded' (Gallacher and Gallagher, 2008). Some educationalists and childhood researchers are involving younger children and supporting children to lead their own research (Kellett et al., 2004).

Wherever there are socially excluded groups there are moves towards inclusive research. Walmsley (2004, p. 69) helpfully reminds us that 'only the excluded need inclusive research', although I would argue that others also benefit from it. Politically active groups of socially excluded people have often driven the move towards inclusive research (Frankham, 2009), though not every individual wants it. Where there is a culture of service provision, such as with older people, this is more likely to take the form of service evaluation, user-led or user-involved research, or PAR. Users, survivors or resisters of mental health service provision may perceive a need for a radically different approach from conventional research done on them. Similarly, feminist and lesbian, gay, bisexual and transgender (LGBT) groups often want to start from a different conceptual place altogether. Participation has been fundamental in international development and collaboration has underpinned a wealth of PRA, CBPR and PAR (Ackermann et al., 2003; Frankham, 2009).

As Walmsley (2004, p. 69) argues, 'inclusion can, quite appropriately, take different forms' and there is 'no one right way to approach inclusive research'. There is, then, no uniformity to the involvement of lay researchers or those traditionally the subject of other people's research in the research process. They are more likely to be co-researchers in some fields than others. They are more likely to be involved in data collection than in the interpretation and analysis of data (Byrne et al., 2009; Nind, 2011). They are more likely to be funded by some funding bodies than others and published in only a handful of journals (Nind and Vinha, 2012). As Sin and Fong (2010, p. 10) observe, there is a great deal of 'mundane messiness' in research decisions when the terrain, value systems and drivers are complex. While there is no uniformity, however, there is a trend. There is more inclusive research now than a decade ago and more in that decade than the previous. The sustainability and desirability of this trend is explored further in the book, together with what is driving this trend. My intention is to bring to this text, which introduces inclusive research to those who are interested but not expert, a sense of the debates associated with it as well as the practicalities and challenges that have been insufficiently debated in a methodological development still in its relative infancy (Walmsley and Johnson, 2003; Frankham, 2009).

2 Inclusive research as an evolving set of practices

In this second chapter I present inclusive research as an evolving set of practices. I start with the influences that led to researchers explicitly conceptualizing earlier examples of inclusive research as emancipatory, participatory or user-led or user-involved. In this way I put the current diversity in inclusive research into the context of a small number of origins and show the thinking that informed how the diversity developed. Thereby the diversification and application of ideas can be considered in relation to the drivers for researchers to conceptualize, design, conduct and disseminate their research in ways that are more inclusive of the communities their research concerns. This reflects the importance of the context in considering 'what is inclusive research' and it also allows the language of inclusive research, with terms such as 'co-researchers' (Cahill, 2007), 'peer researchers' (Coad and Evans, 2008) and 'children as active researchers'/'child-led research' (Kellett, 2005a), to emerge in those contexts.

The academic context

The context influencing the emergence of inclusive research approaches includes the academic and the wider societal context. I start with the academic and two broad, interrelated spheres of influence within this: the development of qualitative research and the sociology of the 1970s. Some commentators see participatory approaches as developing from qualitative research methodologies highlighting – and problematizing – the hierarchical relationships between researchers and participants and the need to give participants greater voice. French and Swain (1997), for example, reflect on how, with qualitative researchers concerned with listening to and documenting people's voices and experiences, research was extending more and more into seeing things from participants' perspectives. For some, a logical next step was utilizing those perspectives (and people) in the design and conduct of the research. Thus, participatory research is seen as embedded in the qualitative research tradition and linked with the view that 'all knowledge is socially constructed' (p. 26) in contexts which underpin it. In *What is Qualitative Research?*, Hammersley (2013) reminds us of this concern to explore how people understand, experience, interpret, voice and produce their social worlds and the essential role of subjectivity within this. This is nowhere more clearly evident than in collaborative ethnography, an application of ethnography in which researchers and 'subjects' collaborate to produce ethnographic texts (Lassiter, 2005) or in feminist research that seeks to ground research in the actual experiences of women through methods that access these (DuBois, 1983, cited by Lassiter, 2005).

As qualitative research has gained momentum, so too has interest in seeing the world through the eyes of those the research concerns. Indeed, Lassiter (2005) argues that collaborating with the researched has a well-established tradition in applied anthropology where activist roots are evident. Such tendencies in qualitative research to consider 'responsibility to publics outside the academy' (Lassiter, 2005, p. 84), however, have not meant the prescription of a unique set of methods, nor is there consensus that this has been pervasive. While qualitative research has influenced inclusive research, not all inclusive research is qualitative and not all qualitative research has participatory or emancipatory dimensions (Bennett, 2004, cited by Frankham, 2009). Qualitative research, however, has brought with it a concept of research as 'cooperative experiential enquiry' (Reason, 1988; Kiernan, 1999) going beyond the priorities of researchers to those of the ordinarily researched.

If participatory research has roots in qualitative research then emancipatory research, argue French and Swain (1997), has roots in the social model of disability; this social model of disability, in turn, has its roots in the interface of sociology and the voices of disabled people. According to the social model, people are disabled not by their actual impairments but by physical and social barriers in the environment; the research agenda becomes focused on people's experience of those physical and social barriers, thereby challenging them. Thus, emancipatory research may be seen as less of a methodology and more as a 'part of the struggle of disabled [and other marginalized] people to control the decision-making processes that shape their lives' (p. 27). (Readers particularly interested in this field will be interested to note that French and Swain went on to develop their own, alternative, 'affirmative model'.) The essence of the social model has more recently been applied to socially excluded groups, older people and users of mental health services (Warren and Boxall, 2009), people with learning difficulties (Bjornsdottir and Svensdottir, 2008) and those involved with alcohol misuse and its treatment (Staddon, 2012), each seeking to reframe their understanding of their situations. To various degrees, these groups have developed a commitment to mutual support and empowering them-selves individually and collectively including through their involvement in research (Frankham, 2009). In this way, much inclusive research has been motivated by a drive to redress wrongs, both past and present; for aca-demics this means responding to the 'call to discard our colonizing ways, drop the jargon, reject "rejecting research" and put ourselves and our skills at the disposal of people with learning difficulties [and others] so that they might take their rightful place in charge of the research agenda' (Walmsley, 2004, p. 66). Here inclusive research has developed as the antidote to the bulk of the research *done to* people which is experienced as oppressive – research being 'one of the dirtiest words in the indigenous world's vocabu-lary' (Smith, 2012, p. xi). 'People who have pioneered the work have done so because they want to change things, to show that in the small world of research we can do things differently, and better' (Walmsley, 2004, p. 69).

While sociologists of disability challenged the ways in which disabled people were conceptualized, with repercussions for how disability research was conceptualized, this pattern is also evident in the field of childhood. A changing model of childhood emerged in the 1990s and, with echoes of what happened in relation to disability, this led to 'a shift from a focus on the child as *object of* to a focus on the child as *subject* (and actor) *in* research' (Mason and Danby, 2011, p. 185). The new social studies and discourse of childhood connected with a rights discourse to bring about a 'participatory rights perspective' (Dockett and Perry, 2011, p. 232), which fostered a significant rise in participatory research with children. More recently this extended into pushes for research led *by* children (Kellett, 2005a). The theoretical conceptualization of children as active meaning makers capable of co-constructing knowledge has been influential in this context.

While children were not calling for more control over research prac-tices in the way that disabled people were, this 'insistent voice' has been strongly heard among feminist and critical race theorists (Frankham, 2009, p. 2). Bowles and Duelli Klein (1983), for example, saw the need for dialogic research accounts that would better represent women's diverse experiences; the vehicle would be the academic researcher and the woman researched taking their versions of reality to each other in a transactional process. Reinharz (1992, p. 181) describes feminist participatory research as adopting 'an approach of openness, reciprocity, mutual disclosure, and shared risk'. Indeed feminist research, premised on 'the personal is political', has been influential in supporting notions of research being linked to the struggle of oppressed groups to gain 'full citizenship' (French and Swain, 1997, p. 31) and to the core idea that 'research should contribute to women's liberation' (Acker et al., 1991, p. 131, cited by Danieli and Woodhams, 2005). It is perhaps here, more than in any other field, that the arguments for the abandonment of the role of researcher as expert in relation to the researched have raged and led to change (Reinharz, 1983; Danieli and Woodhams, 2005).

Not all the academic drivers for inclusive research are as principled or conceptually and theoretically oriented as the ones I have discussed here. There may be more pragmatic reasons for the increased interest in participatory methods, as ways of getting data from children or disabled people, for example, when other methods are inadequate. Edwards and Alexander (2011, p. 272) discuss the functional, instrumental benefits that community researchers offer to academic researchers with their 'privileged access' to networks and knowledge. Crow (2010) similarly postulates about the pragmatic considerations at work for researchers who need the participation of social groups and whose participation in research is otherwise difficult to secure. Interest in democratizing research, he argues, may also have been piqued by the increased value in academic circles placed on making impact outside of academic life. Technological advances, too, have played their part in making it possible to generate affordable, high-impact material such as video and disseminate it via the internet. Although this may have flourished in recent years, participatory video practices remain relatively understudied and evaluated (White, 2003; High, 2010).

The wider context influencing the emergence of inclusive research approaches

Inevitably academic debates are situated in wider contexts, and beyond the boundaries of academe other developments have made the rise of inclusive research timely. There is a strong history of social movements influencing inclusive research approaches (see Chevalier and Buckles'

(2013) chapter on action research history for an overview). Globally action research and PAR, for example, have influenced political activists as well as professional researchers, providing an underpinning social justice perspective. What people may now see as largely methodological has been, and in some circles continues to be, more strongly positioned as political (Carr and Kemmis, 2009) and as practical philosophy (Elliott, 2009) concerned with action or social justice (Griffiths, 2009). Concerns with social reform and community development have driven the more critical action research and emancipatory research. Grass roots organizations have been major drivers informing the development of ideas about collaborative, co-produced knowledge for change.

The interest in the democratization of research 'can be seen as part of what some commentators regard as a wider turn to democracy in society' (Edwards and Alexander, 2011, p. 271). In the global arena there has been an increased emphasis on a formal policy process for protecting people's rights reflected in, for example, the United Nations Convention on the Rights of the Child (1989) and the United Nations Convention on the Rights of Persons with Disabilities (2006). The emphasis on 'full inclusion and participation in the community' (United Nations Convention on the Rights of Persons with Disabilities, 2006, Article 19) has been translated into a drive towards the involvement of users of social care and similar services in the management of their services.

Often there has been a logical progression from more participation in service training and service evaluation to people's involvement in other kinds of research (Frankham, 2009). Personal histories of a lack of such involvement and of poor experiences of services helped to drive this forward (Beresford and Carr, 2012), in keeping with moves to use participatory appraisal approaches in international development to give voice to local communities. Moreover, increasingly 'research is grounded in and generated from the complex, entangled situations that comprise the actual challenges confronting communities and policy-makers' and 'emanates not from within the confines of academic disciplines, but rather from the lived experiences of community members and from the policy knots that bind legislative and executive responses' (CCREC, n.d.). In the United Kingdom, amid a climate of growing self-advocacy and growing understanding of the complexity of social problems, the Joseph Rowntree Foundation has led the way by beginning to take on a commitment to funding research in which lay people have had an increasing say in defining research priorities and in the detail and conduct of the research itself.

It is easy to see how this mix of influences, each often adding weight to another, has underpinned the rationale of a multitude of inclusive research projects. Neoliberal new managerialism has provided a context for user-centred research to develop from user involvement in services, whereas disability rights campaigns have provided a context for a differently conceived approach. Holland et al. (2008, pp. 3–4) pin down three dominant lines of argument from analysis of the literature about participatory research and its context. They cleverly define these as: 'rights' (i.e. rights agendas producing a political and legal environment encouraging more participatory approaches), 'right on' (i.e. an implied ethical and moral superiority associated with research that reflects this environment) and the 'right thing to do' (related to methodological arguments about producing 'better' data and research products).

Core ideas in evolving inclusive research practices

Disrupting the hierarchy

I now discuss the core ideas coming from the contextual influences set out earlier and their impact on the development of inclusive research practices. The idea and practice of disrupting the perceived hierarchy of the powerful researcher and the powerless researched is important within and beyond the academy, both with methodologists and politicized emancipatory researchers. This language of disruption was used by Smith (2012, p. x):

> I wrote *Decolonizing Methodologies* primarily to disrupt relationships between researchers (mostly non indigenous) and researched (indigenous), between a colonizing institution of knowledge and colonized peoples whose own knowledge was subjugated.

Reinharz (1992, p. 181) similarly refers to feminist participatory research seeking to achieve 'an egalitarian relation'. One example of this is Lykes' (1989) positioning of her research with Guatemalan women as communal rather than hierarchical. Todd (2012, p. 95) discusses how 'researching with children involves "queer(ing) the relationship between the researcher and the researched" (McClelland and Fine, 2008) in order to "rupture . . . the ordinary" (Leitch et al. 2007).' Warren and Boxall (2009, p. 293) reflect on their desire to open up the academy with its hierarchical structures and self-interests to disrupt the dichotomy between 'those who teach and research v. those who are taught and researched'. This focus on who holds the power is sometimes travelling in new directions and developing new epistemological positions. It can be about democratization and mild discomfort with the traditional assignment of roles and privilege. Equally, it can be about anger and revulsion at the ways in which researchers have used their power over the researched to label and reject them (Townson et al., 2004), medicalize and pathologize them (Beresford and Wallcraft, 1997), or colonize them (hooks, 1990).

This concern with the power dynamic is, as one would expect, mobilized into action differently across the range of inclusive research. There can be a notion of handing power over to children, service users, and so on, as if power were a commodity that can be passed around. Thus, in participatory approaches there is a discourse about children and service users being given the power to conduct the interviews or to choose their preferred method(s). Alternatively, there can be a sense of sharing power, as in PAR in which the different communities involved seek sufficient openness to listening to each other to work towards a common purpose, or there can be a sense of seizing power by seizing control of the agenda for the research, as some groups of disabled people and mental health service survivors have done. Foucault (1989), however, maintains that power is exercised rather than possessed and the detailed examples in Chapter 3 illustrate this exercising of power at work in various research projects.

Maximizing participation and competence

Somewhat different to the focus on the power dynamic between researcher and researched is the focus on participation at a more basic level, this being intrinsic to inclusion in social, political and civic life: 'The need for meaningful involvement of disabled people and other commonly marginalised groups is increasingly accepted across policy, service planning and delivery, and research' (Sin and Fong, 2010, p. 13). This core idea is particularly important in opening up research to all and translates into developing more inclusive methods. As Booth and Booth (1996, p. 67) argue, 'too often the potential problems of interviewing inarticulate subjects are seen in terms of their deficits rather than the limitations of our methods' and therefore 'serves to legitimate' their exclusion from research. Their use of photovoice with people with learning difficulties to enable them to share their experiences of being parents is an example of addressing this barrier to participation.

Porter et al. (2012, p. 131) reflect on the developments following the UN rights conventions, with young people's proactive participation in research promoted and fostered by child-focused non-governmental organizations (NGOs) and academics. This has translated into young people working in collaboration with organizations like Save the Children and supported by, for example, the Children's Research Centre at the Open University in England, planning and conducting their own research. Children and young people are increasingly involved in policy evaluation with the idea that this benefits the policy process and the young people as citizens (Fisher and Robinson, 2010). This may seem very tame, civilizing as much as empowering, but it reflects a significant shift from a position of people being seen as barely fit subjects for study to that of making a worthwhile contribution.

The debate about the competence of lay people, particularly children and people with learning disabilities, to do research has shifted as real projects have extended people's expectations. Thomas and O'Kane (1998, p. 346) argue that, 'rather than reinforce views of children's incompetence by portraying them as victims, we have to develop methods which allow us to explore children's capacities, needs and interests from their own point of view.' Inclusive research at its most basic, then, is about demonstrating people's competence to hold and give their perspectives and their growing status as social actors who do not need to be dealt with by proxies. The skill of researchers to 'tune in' and 'adjust our listening' (Clark, 2001, p. 333) has shown the ability of even very young children to contribute to research. In inclusive research, which 'is no longer the exclusive province of the "expert"', 'expertise and skills are shared collaboratively' (Johnson, 2009, p. 252).

Kellett (2005a, p. 7) puts less emphasis on traditional researchers enhancing their skills as facilitators in the research process, or on collaborative skill-sharing, and more emphasis on teaching children the skills of academic research. From her early action research to explore the potential of such training she became 'extremely positive about the ability of children as young as ten to undertake rigorous, empirical research and the impact of such participation on child self-development'. She has developed and widely promoted four models of training for children to become researchers, and (echoing the social model of disability) she argues that it is scepticism about children's competence as researchers that has been the main barrier. She also maintains that child researchers are now seen as different to, rather than lesser than, adult researchers (Kellett, 2011, p. 207). A similar argument is made by Lou Townson, an experienced researcher with learning disabilities, about the barrier of low expectations faced by, and challenged by, the research groups she has been involved with (Nind and Vinha, 2012). Proponents of inclusive research such as Warren and Boxall (2009) see the failure of professionals and academics to recognize the competence of, for example, older people and their capability for full, equal partnership as presenting an ongoing problem.

Jones et al. (2012, p. 1) describe their desire to work with underrepresented voices in educational inquiry and to seek 'an inclusive lens'. They see their book on the Accessible Research Cycle (ARC) as offering 'a way to support teachers to generate and complete research about their own practice; thereby becoming the initiators and owners of the research' (p. 3). Focused more on teachers than learners, they discuss the tension of their being both users and generators of research evidence and the importance of viewing themselves as 'capable inquirers into their own practice' (p. 4). As with Kellett's (2005b) book on teaching research methods to children, they attempt a codification of process, in this case scaffolding the research process for practitioners and seeking to make it jargon-free to bring research closer to practice. Not all attempts to bring research skills to lay people are so prescriptive, however, and implicit rather than explicit approaches to building research expertise are in use (Nind, 2011).

The rise of inclusive research is inextricably linked with the rise of concerns about people having a voice and making a difference. The involvement of lay people in health research 'reflects the policy drive for greater accountability . . . and is based on the assumption that it will lead to services which are of better quality and more relevant to the needs of patients' (Ross et al., 2005, p. 269). Inclusive research practices therefore encompass a range of work enhancing, sharing and teaching research skills, including the skills related to managing the diverse voices involved. Walmsley, writing with Central England People First (in press), reflects on how self-advocate Simone Aspis (2000) used the powerful maxim of 'Nothing about us without us' 'to challenge the right of non disabled people to have any say in the history of learning disabilities'. Until the pioneering inclusive research of the social history of learning disabilities group at the Open University, this had largely been the province of non-disabled academics. The 'nothing about us without us' message reached Anne

McGuire, then Minister for Disabled People in England, who has stressed talking to and involving disabled people (Sin and Fong, 2010). Similarly Kellett (2010, p. 32), referring to Thorne (2002), argues that 'children and young people have been silenced historically in the accounts of sociologists, historians and anthropologists all of whom claim to speak with their voice'. The field of inclusive research therefore has been fraught with arguments about who can speak for whom, and often a resistance to the idea that the voices of those traditionally researched by others being mediated by others (e.g. Kellett, 2010).

The question of participation and the purpose it serves is addressed by Lassiter (2005, p. 84) in his discussion of collaborative ethnography/ anthropology. Here participation is about working 'side-by-side' for mutual benefit. Participation in the research, he argues, is not just about 'giving back', but about 'give and take' in the sharing of expertise and 'fully dialogic exchange of knowledge'. In CBPR the 'ideological rationale [is] framed in terms of an explicit value position involving a commitment to sharing power . . . and to working for progressive social change' (Durham Community Research Team, 2011, p. 3); an emphasis placed on the research being 'more egalitarian and democratic, based on respect for and partnership with community members' (p. 6).

Enhancing authenticity

The democratization of research brings with it the democratization of knowledge and the questioning of what is authoritative knowledge and what is legitimate knowledge (Durham Community Research Team, 2011; Edwards and Alexander, 2011). Another core idea among proponents of inclusive research, then, is that it can, and does, produce more authentic knowledge (Grover, 2004; Reason and Bradbury, 2008). This is the idea that knowledge is more authentic, valid even, when grounded in the experiences and values of those concerned. This idea is strong in moves for child-led research and Kellett (2011, p. 211) explicitly states, 'the power of child-child research is that it can transcend inequalities in power dynamics and propagate authentic insider perspectives'. This reflects the notion that 'children are experts on their own lives', privileged as insiders to childhood, or when they are disabled or living in traveller communities, enjoying 'double' insider status (p. 212). The logic here is that one's identity brings with it a particular view of the world based in that identity, which in turn produces a particular kind of knowledge. Porter et al. (2012, p. 132) observe that children are sought as co-investigators based on the premise that 'knowledge about children may best be produced by them'. For Thomas and O'Kane, (1998, p. 341), 'children's own understandings of their situation may be as valid as any other' but, for Kellett, children's own understandings are more valid because, 'with regard to childhood itself – in the sense of what it is like to be a child – it is children who have the expert knowledge' (Kellett, 2005a, p. 9). One view is that children's participation in the interpretation of data can enhance validity (Thomas and O'Kane, 1998) and the other view is that it is essential to validity. The underpinning assumptions here are fiercely critiqued, as I show in Chapter 4, with one counter-view being that people are not best placed to know themselves. The wider academic debates about insider/outsider research and the value of making the familiar strange are pertinent here.

Authenticity arguments can focus on who does the analysis and who authors the knowledge. For some the best knowledge comes from co-production or, as Lassiter (2005, p. 96) puts it, 'cointerpretation is what ultimately makes an ethnography collaborative'. For others co-production is inferior to community-controlled knowledge production (Durham Community Research Team, 2011). ICPHR (2013, p. 13) see participatory health research as characterized by producing knowledge which is 'local, collective, co-created, dialogical and diverse'. Arguments about inclusive research producing more authentic knowledge, however, rest not just on the importance of the involvement of children or other marginalized or oppressed people/participants in providing and analysing data, but on the importance of their involvement in shaping questions. Working collaboratively, for example, focused on the concerns of practitioners, can mean that the 'reality' gaps between them and academics are bridged (Fergusson, 2012, p. 125). For Torre and Fine (2006, cited by Cahill, 2007, p. 298) involving people usually marginal to setting the agenda is important because of the depth of their knowledge and, for Torre et al. (2001), because of its unique quality; 'insiders "simply know things that outsiders don't"'. Cahill (2007) suggests that these authors do not confuse deep, insider knowledge with 'the truth', but that they highlight the potential for new lines of vision. For Holland et al. (2008) and Fenge (2010) participatory approaches incorporating such multiple perspectives can create understandings that are more holistic, and for Burke and Kirton (2006, p. 2, cited by Jones et al., 2012, p. 1) involving insider, local perspectives can lead to more 'nuanced and complex understandings'.

A further argument about authenticity is based on what knowledge has previously been privileged and what neglected. Often experiential knowledge has been valued for its authenticity, but still allocated a lower status than other knowledge or evidence (Beresford and Carr, 2012). Thus, authenticity is enhanced when the approaches 'access and valorise previously neglected knowledges and provide more nuanced understandings of complex social phenomena' (Kesby, 2000, p. 423). There is seen to be a correspondence between democratizing knowledge production and increasing the validity of data (Kitchen, 2000). Many qualitative researchers are concerned with checking the validity of their data, through member checking, for example, allowing for misunderstandings to be identified and fixed and for constructs to be credible. Cho and Trent (2006), however, propose that an alternative to this transactional validity process is a transformational validity process involving more fundamentally changed relationships. As with Lather's 'catalytic validity', validity processes should empower and emancipate and 'the researcher should openly express how his or her own subjectivity has progressively been challenged and thus transformed as he or she collaboratively interacts with his or her participants' (Cho and Trent, 2006, p. 332). In this way it is not just participants'/ co-researchers' capacity to perceive differently (and our need to learn from their firsthand, direct experience) that matters, but their capacity to make a difference to their worlds.

Empowerment

The idea of authenticity leads to the idea of empowerment. A central premise in inclusive research is that 'those who have in the past so often been the mere objects of investigation, themselves become the agents of their own transformation' (Fielding, 2004, p. 306). There is a good deal written about how 'the interests of children and young people, as a relatively powerless group, are served when they set their own agendas and lead their own research' (Kellett, 2005a, p. 6). The outcomes for children are said to be self-development, political agency, increased confidence and self-esteem, in turn leading to more active participation by children in other aspects affecting their lives' (p. 10). The evidence for this active citizenship happening in practice is sparse, as yet. In the field of learning disabilities it is those people who are already involved in organized self-advocacy who become researchers and so the nature of this relationship, if there is one, may be in the other direction. Cahill (2007) argues that describing the engagement of young people in research as building their capacity for analysis and transformation may be a safer assertion than saying that they are actually analysing and becoming transformed. Indeed, involvement in the research process can be important for enhancing people's understanding of the barriers and enablers for their participation (Johnson, 2009), whatever they do with that understanding.

One of the key differences between children's involvement in the research process and the involvement of self-advocates/service users is that the former are likely to be involved as individuals and the latter as groups. This individual/group dynamic is important in that French and Swain (1997, p. 28) argue that 'emancipation of a group of people can further the empowerment of individuals just as empowerment of individuals can further the emancipation of a group'. The claim that participating in the conduct of research can be empowering and transformative beyond the realms of research reflects a particular view of participatory democracy as much as a reality. In the field of learning disabilities, for example, the engagement of learning disabled people in doing research has expanded the horizons of those individuals and enriched their lives, as well as sometimes changing things for other people with learning disabilities; nonetheless, structural barriers to their active citizenship and to careers in research remain immense (Nind and Vinha, 2012).

The debate about whether, and how, inclusive research empowers is for some people part of a wider debate about its impact in a wider sense. Staley (2009) has explored the impact of public involvement in health research in the United Kingdom for the organization INVOLVE, primarily because this development is founded on a rights argument about involvement, but raises the question of whether it actually makes a difference. In a tight economic climate, interest in evidence demonstrating the added value of an inclusive approach increases in importance. Staley notes the limited evidence available for judging impact and the difficulty in assessing it. Nonetheless, her literature review shows how researchers have been empowered to ask more relevant questions, design more accessible and meaningful studies and engage underrepresented groups. Moreover, the literature shows how the public have benefited from acquiring new knowledge and skills, developing personally, gaining in many ways, but also sometimes being emotionally burdened, overloaded, exposed or frustrated. Communities may gain credibility and recognition for their contribution and build important new alliances. Maximizing positive impact (and perhaps empowerment and transformation) appears to depend on 'involvement throughout a research project, long-term involvement, training and support for the people involved, [and] linking involvement to decision-making' (Staley, 2009, p. 84).

Accessibility, authorship and readership

The core question of who the research is for relates not just to who benefits from it in the sense of positive impacts, but also to who can access it. Thus, evolving inclusive research processes centre on the audience for research knowledge as well as the producers of research knowledge. The principle of accessibility of the research question, research process and research products is a defining one for inclusive research, according to Walmsley and Johnson (2003). Similarly, Van Blerk and Ansell (2007, p. 314) argue that feedback to research participants and dissemination to wider policy and practice audiences both need to be 'active and participatory, where researchers engage with participants and practitioners', rather than 'passive, where the researchers take the lead'. Moreover, they argue that the discourse regarding participatory feedback and dissemination is underdeveloped and, with notable exceptions, passive approaches still dominate. This issue has though received particular attention in PRA and in research involving people with learning disabilities. Accessible products of research include plain English or 'easyread' reports and alternatives to the written word such as multimedia outputs including exhibitions, live drama productions and videos shared via the internet (Nind and Vinha, 2012).

For lay people involved in doing research, their relationships with the products of the research are important for a range of reasons. Writing research reports and papers may not have the same currency for career development outside of the academy, but not doing so can keep lay researchers on the outside. Authorship, or ownership, is an important way of people being credentialized through research (Warren and Boxall, 2009) and without it they can feel used or made inferior (McClimens, 2008). Yet, as Holland et al. (2008) warn, involving participants in dissemination can also lead to somewhat sanitized research stories being told because involving participants who know each other's identities precludes telling personal narratives about them. This whole area of authorship was a sensitive topic among the researchers in focus groups I have facilitated where learning disabled people were just breaking new ground in becoming peer-reviewers as well as editors of a journal special issue (see *British*

Journal of Learning Disabilities, 2012 special issue). Similarly, researchers working collaboratively with children have reflected on the challenge of getting published papers co-written with them (Nind et al., 2012). It may be that Lassiter's (2005) distinction between co-authoring and co-writing is helpful here, that is, participants or co-researchers can shape and influence a text without necessarily writing any of the words that appear in the final version of a research report, paper or ethnographic text. Lassiter recognizes the power issues here and also that not all collaborative research is equitable and good natured, which can make co-authorship difficult. In my experience, the terrain of who authors/writes and how in/accessible texts are made can be the battlegrounds of inclusive research.

Ethical considerations

As I alluded to when referring to Holland et al.'s (2008) reference to 'rights, right on and the right thing to do', one of the core arguments adopted by inclusive researchers is around ethics and an assumption of ethical superiority. This reflects the essential premise that inclusive research is respectful (Cornwall and Jewkes, 1995; Walmsley and Johnson, 2003). The Durham Community Research Team (2011, p. 2) acknowledge this claim to greater inherent ethics in CBPR compared with so-called traditional research, because it is 'more ethically-aware' and sensitive to issues of power, rights and responsibilities and 'more egalitarian and democratic' (p. 6). They set out to move beyond such assumptions to explore the distinctive ethical challenges and to draft ethical principles and guidelines for CBPR in the United Kingdom. They show how ethics is fundamental to inclusive researchers. Similarly, Zeni (2009) argues that the engaged nature of action research changes the ethics dimension so that it is the ethical standards of accountability, action for social justice, and caring and respect that become foregrounded and personal.

For Thomas and O'Kane (1998), a participatory approach in their research with children is important not just for its reliability and validity but for its ethical acceptability. They see giving children some control over the research process as an ethical course of action and part of addressing the disparities in power between children and adult researchers and the challenges associated with gatekeepers and overprotection. Smith (2012, pp. x–xi) writes of working to develop research approaches 'that addressed the stinging criticisms being made by my own communities about the unethical, individualistic practice of research that in their view often rewarded researchers for telling half-truths or downright lies, that misrepresented our world, and that gave authority about us to academic researchers'.

Holland et al. (2008), however, learning from their own research involving young people, remind us of the complexities at work. They conclude that adopting a participatory approach is *a*, rather than *the*, right or helpful thing to do, not least because of the positive ethical framework in which it is embedded. Nonetheless, they also argue that it is not always ethical for children and young people to have power over each other or to analyse each other's data even if they are interested in doing so, which they may well not be. Acting ethically requires a critical reflexivity which may be challenging for some people who have not always been treated well themselves (Conolly, 2008), though Kellett (2005a) maintains that the child researchers she has trained have had no problems with ethical practice. Despite these uncertainties and differences in interpretation or detail, what is clear is that the drive for inclusive research is a drive for ethical research (Nind et al., 2012).

Ethics, then, have been at the forefront of people's concerns as inclusive research practices have evolved. The published ethics frameworks of research councils and learned societies are not always well suited to the more extreme changes associated with emancipatory/user-led research. We now see university ethics committees grappling not just with how to protect groups they see as vulnerable in the research process, but how to adjust to what it means when these people themselves occupy the status of researcher. The discourses around what is risky and safe are being challenged and, rather than understanding people to be either powerful or vulnerable, various competing interests need to be understood in a more fluid and nuanced way. Having the subjects/users of research redefine themselves as doers of research can be disconcerting, even challenging, and it can be tempting for these new researchers to test out what it feels like to be powerful. New marginal voices or groups can be created, or old ones re-created, in the power plays that transpire. The evolution of inclusive research practices can be ethical or perilous, or a mixture of the two!

Summary

There are core ideas that are important to researchers adopting more inclusive approaches. These ideas about power, participation, authenticity, empowerment, accessibility and ethics represent common concerns. When it comes to the detail and practicalities, though, the core ideas are interpreted differently, influenced in part by disciplinary backgrounds, fields of knowledge, the nature of the participants/researchers and the socio-cultural contexts. Also influential is the limited time these developments have had to mature and to be subjected to ongoing scrutiny.

3 Inclusive research: Stories from the field

In a book about the nature of a particular kind of research there is a strong role for examples that illustrate ideas in action. Chapters 1 and 2 indicate the diversity of concepts and evolving practices encompassed within inclusive research approaches. In this chapter, I illustrate some of the ways that inclusive research is practised. To organize the examples in a simplified way I use the framework of:

1. examples of research led by lay researchers/user groups,
2. examples of research conducted in partnership between academics and lay researchers/user groups,
3. examples of research by academics designed to enhance the active participation of participants/user groups.

I deliberately include examples from different fields and disciplines and select those that give the reader insights into the researchers' thinking as well as actions. I end the chapter with some thoughts about how the skills of inclusive research are taught and learned.

Lay researcher-led research

As I have discussed, for some, lay researcher-led research is the pinnacle of inclusive research. In this section, I present examples that illustrate the diversity of research that can be termed lay-researcher led. This diversity encompasses rationales, types of research and the methods used. I have subdivided this section into three examples of research projects that challenge the system, one example of self-advocacy research, and a section describing and discussing child-led research.

User-led research challenging the system

My first set of examples comes from groups using (or resisting) services, as these often engage in research that challenges those services or that reflects a fundamentally different perspective. To illustrate this point I present three projects here, focusing on their raison d'être: one led by psychiatric system survivors, one led by women survivors of alcohol misuse and one led by a community group for people who are LGBT.

Research by psychiatric system survivors can be driven by revulsion at traditional research done *on* them, which they experience as invasive and exploitative (Beresford and Wallcraft, 1997). Understandably, projects like the National User Involvement Project (Lindlow, 1996, cited by Beresford and Wallcraft, 1997) represent a resistance to being researched by people holding power over them. Beresford and Wallcraft (1997, p. 801) explain:

> Sharp differences between survivor-led research and that carried out by mental health professionals are often revealed in the choice of starting point, subject matter and perspective. While psychiatric researchers generally evaluate existing orthodox psychiatric interventions from an assumption that mental illness can be clinically defined, survivor-led research often treats the concept of mental illness as open to question. While the findings of orthodox research generally point to incremental changes within the existing paradigm, user-led research posits more radical shifts of control, rights, knowledge and resources to service users and their organizations.

The different starting point is evident in Staddon's (2012) emancipatory research with women survivors of alcohol issues and their treatment, which was planned with other women in the same position as her. She was, she explains, 'very aware already that our ways of seeing were quite different from those of the so-called experts in the field' (p. 195). She reflects on how the women were put in touch with each other through focus groups, and how: 'If I had not been a service user, as well as a researcher, if the research Advisory Group had not been made up of service users – perhaps nothing more would have come from these meetings. But the pain and anger of these women resonated with us all' (p. 196). The research experience led to the women continuing to meet as a regular network and, greatly influenced by the social model of disability, to theorize afresh and develop a social model of alcohol 'misuse' focused on social components and recognizing the blame culture in services. The 'core component' of the group 'was the refusal to judge or be judged, and to challenge morally and medically informed critiques of their lives' (p. 199).

Count Me in Too, the LGBT community-led project (Browne et al., 2012), involved partnership working from the beginning stage of designing the research, setting out to 'empower marginalized LGBT people, and yet still contribute to the agendas of those "in power"' (p. 205). The PAR approach 'meant contesting traditional divides between community, university and the public sector' (p. 207) with key stakeholders working together 'to generate useful data, crossing and blurring boundaries between activism, service provision, researcher, community member, LGBT, cisgendered [i.e. 'those whose gender assignment at birth continues to be the gender that they identify with and live with'], heterosexual etc' (pp. 208–9). Browne et al. (2012) reflect on the importance of marginalized people sitting down together with powerful people to effect social change. It was this, rather than the mix of research methods they adopted, that made their research powerful.

User-led research: The history of self-advocacy

These examples are very telling regarding what was valued about the research by those involved in conducting it – the *why* – yet they tell very little about the detail of the *how* – what conducting the research inclusively involved. I now turn, therefore, to a more detailed example of research led by lay people who are usually the focus of other people's research. The research was conducted by members of Central England People First (CEPF), a self-advocacy group of people with learning disabilities that has been together for 21 years, with experience of several research projects. The particular study was of the history of self-advocacy focusing on the CEPF group in particular, motivated by their desire to consider and celebrate their journey as individuals and together, especially in light of an apparent decline in self-advocacy groups and members. The paper reporting the research is in the public domain (Walmsley and CEPF, in press) and group members also spoke about their research in the *Doing Research Inclusively, Doing Research Well?* study in which inclusive researchers came together to explore quality in inclusive research (Nind and Vinha, 2012, 2013).

Walmsley spells out exactly who led the history of self-advocacy research:

> This was an inclusive research project. It met all the criteria for inclusive research set by Walmsley and Johnson (2003). Members

of CEPF actively chose to do the project, were in charge of key decisions and carried out much of the work. It was a team approach. Non disabled people played a hugely significant role, as supporters, advisors and expert consultants – it could not have happened without them – but decisions remained in the hands of the CEPF project team. In this sense it demonstrates the viability of an inclusive research approach to a substantial project. (Walmsley and CEPF, in press)

The self-advocates reiterate their role as lead researchers: 'CEPF has always made sure people with learning difficulties run things, so the project was led by one of our members, Craig Hart, supported by the Project Worker, and 7 CEPF members – Ian, Mark, Angela, Stephen, John, Philip and Louise.' What is illuminative for our purposes in understanding the nature of inclusive research is that they are very explicit about who did what in the research process. This is something that Walmsley (2004), working with them on the research, has argued for as necessary to the credibility and sustainability of inclusive research. This transparency is further enhanced by their experimentation with using different fonts in the paper to indicate whose ideas are being voiced at any one time – who is speaking – though they acknowledge that the ownership of many key ideas was shared. The paper explains that, while the self-advocates recorded the history of their group, Walmsley – the academic – wrote the history of self-advocacy. The self-advocates explain that 'this was because we have not read the books and papers that Jan Walmsley had read'. They expand further:

> For professionals and other important people we need to influence we needed to write something that helped explain self advocacy. We knew that they might want more detail than would normally be in an easy read document. This was a difficult decision but we decided that with help we could write something that we couldn't write by ourselves but that we could understand. (Walmsley and CEPF, in press)

Echoing all of the inclusive researchers participating in our reflective focus groups (Nind and Vinha, 2012), this group's story of their research approach is one of compromises in which pragmatics are held in delicate balance with principled decisions. Unable to write the bigger story themselves, the group engaged a trusted academic researcher to do this part, thus showing that research led by lay people does not have to be fully conducted by them. They tell the story of coming to the decision that they could not do the whole thing themselves and to bid for funds for a project worker with oral history skills to work with them as well as to buy in equipment and website expertise, and to fund a booklet, exhibition and workshops 'for our members to help them learn about archives, oral history, interviewing, website development, scanning, Skype, and writing up what we found' (Walmsley and CEPF, in press).

The study was funded by the Heritage Lottery Fund and the research was conducted while the group were at the same time working hard to seek other funds for their own organizational survival. The research methods included interviewing key people in the organization's history, building a photographic log and photo stories of the history of the group, and building a timeline of key events. Particular challenges arose around deciding the best response to the ethical dilemmas surrounding interpersonal troubles ('battles') in the group dynamic. Some, but not all of the interviewing was done by people with learning disabilities. This compromise was an originally unanticipated result of the sensitivities that transpired regarding interviewing people known to each other with shared pasts and not always enough distance between them for comfort (an experience similarly reported by Grant, 2013).

This study was research in which hearing, rather than seamlessly blending, the different voices was very important. The self-advocates explain:

> We have always debated whether support workers should have their own voice, and on the whole we have said they shouldn't. We sorted this by doing an interview with the support worker and putting it on the website. We also included some of the things he thought were important in the Timeline and the booklet. So his voice is there too, alongside ours. That seemed fair. (Walmsley and CEPF, in press)

Experienced at understanding diverse needs they organized the booklet reporting the research so that, when open, one page was in the academic's words and the page alongside it was in the words of the self-advocates. The fact that not everything was fully accessible was also a compromise – the controversial nature of which the research team fully understood in a conscious decision, carefully deliberated: 'We were not keen to have things which were not in easy read, but we understand that sometimes it is important to make exceptions to our rules' (Walmsley and CEPF, in press).

The findings from this research are testimony to the 'personal is political' fundamental premise. They show a history with periods of expansion and retraction as well as personal and group triumphs. The paper, which focuses on the research process as well as products, also demonstrates the power of doing the research for providing those involved with fresh insights into their past, their current situation and possible futures.

Child-led research

I now turn to examples of research led by less experienced but more formally trained researchers, that is, by children. The contrast between these and earlier examples serve to illuminate the diversity in research led by lay researchers. Kellett's (2005b) book codifying the process of developing children as researchers includes the training she takes children through at the Children's Research Centre and three accounts of research by children. These illustrate the traditional research processes the children underwent, as well as those missed such as reviewing the literature and locating the knowledge generated within the wider field. They show how the children's studies are inevitably motivated by their interests rather more than reflection on their life experiences and personal–political concerns evident in the research accounts of marginalized adults. Perhaps influenced by Kellett's strong view that adults should not interfere, they also lack the sense of combining the skills of individuals from different backgrounds. Thus, these appear to be a mix of school project and conventional research on a very small scale.

Paul O'Brien looked at how experience of death of a relative or pet affected children of his age at his school. This pupil (from Year 7) identified participants through a survey and then did short follow-up interviews with eight of them. Using processes taught through Kellett's approach he was careful to consider the ethics associated with talking about sensitive subjects. He reports the findings question by question and discusses the patterns and diversity he found among interviewees' responses, as well as what doing the research meant to him personally. Unlike the self-advocates discussed, he was a lone researcher and made no attempt to recruit others to do the parts of the research that were beyond his personal skills and the scale of his small, unfunded study, namely the literature review, contextual and theoretical parts.

Ben Davies and Selena Ryan-Vig researched together pupils' views about mixed-gender football, beginning with some analysis of the coverage of men's and women's football in the media and using web searching. Trained in research processes they report on their mixed methods approach comprising a local questionnaire and an experiment involving introducing the experience of mixed-gender football, with observations and follow-up interviews. The child researchers confidently refer to confounding variables and potential bias and discuss the rationale for their main decisions. They present their findings in tables indicating the outcomes of their basic descriptive quantitative analysis and proffer some plausible explanations for patterns in the data. Another duo, Anna Carlini and Emma Barry, report on researching the interactions of peers with school children who were small and looked younger than their chronological age. They did some thematic analysis and reflection on their findings and processes. These research reports by children do not quite portray the sense of them enjoying the emancipation or empowerment seen in other user-led accounts. Nonetheless, there is a strong message about new skills learned and confidence raised.

The various examples of lay researcher-led research highlight the ways in which leading research may involve lay people in challenging, or adopting, traditional research approaches. Lay researchers may recruit academics to do parts of the research or work alone. They may or may not change the way they see themselves and their situations, but they invariably develop new skills and confidence. The outcomes of their research are likely to be different from the outcomes had the research been led by academics.

Partnership research

Partnership research is less focused on who leads and more on how people work together. Sometimes those involved deliberately liberate themselves from constraints imposed by their identity labels. Some but not all partnership research is PAR, but I begin with a PAR example to show how an academic and a group of young women collaborated. This section contains illustrations of highly diverse approaches and methods, all of which can be termed partnership research. The examples of collaborative research projects share something with projects led by lay researchers – the challenge for everyone involved to work out what compromises are acceptable to them. They also illustrate the challenges surrounding who has expertise and ownership, and how to function in unfamiliar roles and unfamiliar relationships. They introduce new terms that are emerging for those roles. 'Learner researchers', 'volunteers' and 'co-learners' emerge as terms alongside 'co-researchers'. Ultimately, this section presents examples of research alliances formed in diverse ways but for a shared purpose of doing research to facilitate changes in people's life situations.

The Makes Me Mad project – an example of deep participatory research

The Makes Me Mad project is interesting because it has the strong political, transformative dimension often associated with user-led research, but without being conducted independently of academic influence. The account is provided by the academic involved and the women's voices are heard through this filter, rather than this being a story jointly told. Cahill (2007) provides a rich example of PAR with young women (aged 16 to 22) in New York, which she describes as deeply participatory, collaborative and reciprocal. They began their work together with an open agenda – the 'everyday lives of young women in the city' (p. 300); ownership of the project was discussed from its inception and the study evolved organically: 'After much deliberation and debate the young women decided to focus our research on the issue of stereotypical (mis)representations of young people of color and the relationship between these images and processes of financial disinvestment from their neighborhood. They entitled the project "Makes Me Mad: Stereotypes of Young Urban Womyn of Color"' (Cahill, 2007, p. 300). Cahill set out to create what Torre (2005) had described as a 'democratic space of radical inclusivity'. Like other inclusive researchers she was influenced by the ideas of Freire and she was highly focused on developing the co-researchers' skills in multiple research methods, not least to help equalize power between them all. She worked to create space for dialogue, which involved 'actively facilitating everyone's involvement', 'interrupting silences' and 'disrupting dominant voices', as well as modelling being an active listener (Cahill, 2007, p. 302). But she is clear that her role transcended being a passive facilitator of others' participation; she was a collaborator, also involved in the research, and also holding opinions. She reflects, 'The key issue however, if one is to participate in ways that do not silence others, is to be very careful about the grounds on which you make a contribution. When I did disagree, I made sure to first clarify I was speaking from my own experience and standpoint, without making any claim to authority' (p. 302).

Cahill (2007) performed a role noticeably absent in the children's independent research discussed earlier, but offered by the academic researcher consulted by CEPF. She supported her co-researchers in making 'connections between participant's interpretations and social and political theory'; she observes, however, that the 'co-researchers soon began to play this role for each other', thereby 'through this process we collectively developed theory' (pp. 302–3). The account of the project makes some of this process explicit. They began with agreeing rules of engagement that enabled them to 'constructively address differences not just consensus' (p. 303). They developed methodological collaborative 'rituals' to support their production of group-owned knowledge (p. 303). After Lather's (1986) 'research as praxis', Cahill refers to their practice as a 'collective praxis approach' (p. 303). Cahill did not opt for the visual methodologies frequently used in participatory research with children and young people to increase engagement and address variation in competence with language and literacy; instead, the group's methods centred on written and verbal expression and the idea of writing as praxis. As well as private journal writing the co-researchers spent time in dialogue and 'note-taking on "our wall"', which produced a 'public memory of shared knowledge production' (p. 303).

I have argued elsewhere that the analysis stage is often the least developed or explicitly discussed in inclusive research, but most developed and inclusive perhaps when 'embedded and boundary-less – part of a broader approach to participation and to acting responsibly' (Nind, 2011, p. 358). I have since learned of many more examples of this and Cahill describes it in their project:

> Moments of analysis emerged organically at multiple and regular points as part of our reflective praxis rather than being a set 'phase' of research. Analysis also fed directly back into our project as part of a looped process of critical reflection. Crucially therefore, the analysis process was not external to the process but an integral part of it in which all the co-researchers participated and learned. (2007, p. 306)

She goes on to consider their processes of actively listening to each other's perspectives and making sense of these as representing a kind of participatory grounded theory 'with the women building an understanding of themselves as they study themselves' (p. 306). She also reports how some aspects of academic research, like intensive collaborative coding, did become points of contention when the co-researchers were not convinced that they were worthwhile.

Researching our lives – an example of participatory data analysis

The previous example is helpful in including an account of the data analysis process as integral to the PAR. I include this next example of partnership research because it is particularly expansive regarding the shared approach to data analysis in which the voice-centred relational method was used. Moreover, it helpfully highlights questions of whether there is an expert in inclusive research conducted collaboratively, or whether this expert role is shared or passed around. In particular it shows how, regardless of the best intentions and careful research methods of the academic researchers, they can still inadvertently dominate decisions about the selection of focus. It also tells of the high levels of sustained commitment to the task and to each other demanded by research involving working together across the stages of research.

Byrne et al. (2009) describe a study involving socio-economically disadvantaged teenagers in Ireland who had left school at the earliest opportunity. The academics engaged in research with a participatory ethos in a team with the teenagers and an artist who they engaged to help them 'to reflect on and research themselves' (p. 70) using film, music and painting. As is so often the case in inclusive research, 'much time was spent clarifying the expectations of all members of the research team in terms of project process, practices and outcomes' (p. 70). Also in common with other inclusive research projects there was an agenda that included learning new skills and potentially leading to wider change – in this case, change in the school system.

Inclusive researchers struggle with voice and language. One challenge is deciding on the term to describe those involved, for which there is no commonly agreed vocabulary. In this study the teenagers are referred to, not as co-researchers, but as 'learner researchers' (p. 71). Another challenge is about how to manage – include and balance – the different voices involved. Byrne et al. (2009, p. 70) selected the voice-centred relational method because it 'offered the possibility of participatory meaning making that emphasized the voices and interests of research participants'. They saw this as a means for analysing interview transcripts collaboratively that would require everyone involved 'to listen attentively to the voice relating the story' (p. 68), to confront difference, and to identify and make the conventions of interpretation explicit. The researchers, including the 'learner researchers', worked on the transcripts methodically and painstakingly in teams and pairs to correct inaccuracies, fill gaps and add to the narrative, persisting despite the 'difficult, tedious and time consuming' (p. 74) nature of the analysis work. Byrne et al. (2009) tell of how at first the academics neglected to see themselves (with their privileged lives) as narrators and as the researched: 'Throughout the project the teenagers had demonstrated that they could be researchers; the academics on the other hand found it difficult to become the researched and step out of the role of expert researcher' (p. 75).

The study of falls – collaborative research with older people

There are many more examples in the literature of inclusive research with young people than older people and I include the next example in part to counter this as well as to show how partnerships can be multidimensional and valued by funders. Ross et al. (2005) reflect on their partnership involving the academic disciplines of nursing, gerontology and geriatrics, with local health and social care providers and the community heath council – the 'consumers'. They joined forces to explore the views of older people, carers, and health and social care professionals on the risk of older people falling. Consumer involvement was a condition of their Department of Health funding and they could access support and training from EQUIP (Effectiveness and Quality in User Involvement Projects) who were specialists in this. They formed a consumer panel of 21 members with diverse experience and concerns and who provided links with other local organizations; this panel worked 'alongside the research team as partners' (p. 270). 'Panel meetings were chaired by the consumer member of the research team. This was important since it helped to establish the panel's identity as a group of consumers separate from, but working alongside, the research team' (p. 271). They needed to be clear that this was worthwhile and not '"just another talking shop"' (p. 274). Consumers were involved in project design, management, analysis and dissemination stages. Ross et al. note the importance of openness in the early stages in which 'it was evident that participants were beginning to set the agenda for the consumer panel, and that panel meetings would need to be flexible to take into account panel members' concerns which were not strictly within the project's remit' (p. 271). Similar to an advisory group, the panel worked to ensure relevance for older people, but they also discussed research methods and got involved with data analysis.

This project is distinctive as an example of collaboration in research not just because of the consumer panel, but because of the role of the research nurse who, in recognition of the challenges in involving older people, eased the development of relationships through careful communication between panel members and between meetings. The research nurse also collated and analysed data from the panel. These data indicated their positive feelings about being involved, not just for their own benefit but in terms of shaping the effectiveness of the recruitment and methods, steering the team away from overprotection and towards speaking appropriately and listening intently. In common with other inclusive researchers, the group found that the role of communication and time to develop research relationships were crucial. Usefully, Ross et al. (2005, p. 273) provide examples of the ways in which older people on the consumer panel made the research participatory, such as one member acting as an independent observer in focus groups and feeding back on 'the appropriateness and consistency of method, facilitation approach, and equity of participation of focus group members'. In another example, the panel joined the researchers in preliminary analysis of interview data to develop a vignette for use in interviews with health and social care professionals.

Collaborative life histories – partnership research in the context of a doctoral thesis

The next example illustrates how research partnerships can be asymmetric in other ways. Here a doctoral researcher, collaborating with young adults with learning disabilities in Iceland, sheds further light on the ways in which expertise and analysis may be tackled in inclusive research collaborations. The account of the research (Bjornsdottir and Svensdottir, 2008) is co-written by the doctoral researcher and one of the young adults involved. They are explicit about how, in co-writing, they spent time in preparation, recording meetings, 'then separately we wrote down our reflections and finally Kristin incorporated all of these into this paper and put our thoughts into context with other writings on the subject of inclusive research. In this paper we want to present a joint voice, which is a product of our collaboration' (p. 265). The concept of joint ideas, if not joint voice, is held in common with the processes and research report by Walmsley and CEPF (in press), but in this case without the people with learning disabilities being in charge. The realities of joint voice, authority and authorship are ones that researchers with learning disabilities and their allies often struggle with (McClimens, 2008).

The research of Bjornsdottir and Svensdottir (2008) comprises the life histories of adults with learning disabilities. They explain the interdependency we have seen in other examples: 'We have done some analysis together; mostly through discussions. Kristin's role is then to place Aileen's story with the other stories into historical and theoretical context' (p. 265). They also reflect on the question of ownership of the research, clarifying that the 'collaborators' (as opposed to co-researchers or learner researchers, the terms used in examples so far) own their own life stories, but Kristin owns her doctoral dissertation. In this complex set of research relationships Kristin is an advocate for disabled people, an ally and, as Shakespeare (1996) suggests, even as a non-disabled person, someone with a stake in disability. Aileen and one of the other people among the six sharing their life stories wanted to be involved in the whole research process. While ultimately Aileen co-authored one part of the dissertation through the inclusion of the paper within it, the product of the research, the ideas and the terminology were not fully accessible. Another non-collaborative element, or compromise in inclusive research terms, was that the people with learning disabilities were not involved in choosing the theoretical framework. Bjornsdottir and Svensdottir (2008, p. 266) reflect: 'We have compared our collaboration with the five criteria of inclusive research set forth by Walmsley and Johnson (2003) and have come to the conclusion that doctoral projects such as this one can most likely never be fully inclusive.'

I include this example, nonetheless, as it illustrates the range of collaborative arrangements and the kinds of study at the edges of partnership research. The politics of inclusive research are still present. People like Aileen sharing life stories are motivated by a desire to prevent repetition of bad things happening and to influence practice. As Bjornsdottir and Svensdottir (2008, p. 266) reflect, Aileen's 'role as a co-researcher and self-advocate are interwoven and driven by the need to be heard (Goodley 2000)'. Less like the examples of the individualized and relatively dispassionate child-led research, and more like PAR, there is a group social responsibility at work here.

Bjornsdottir and Svensdottir (2008) give careful consideration to the question of whether Aileen's involvement in the research was empowering, concluding that seeing the research as the thing that empowered her 'would be an oversimplification of Aileen's life' (p. 266). Nevertheless, they are clear that they 'do not reject the idea of empowerment through research' and that 'we agree that the collaboration has been enjoyable and empowering for both of us' (p. 266). They tell of how spending time together in the research brought them closer and affected the power dynamic between them. They learned how much they had in common, which made the differences between them less of a preoccupation. This is a sentiment echoed by the inclusive researchers with and without a label of learning disability that shared in dialogue in *Doing Research Inclusively, Doing Research Well?* (Nind and Vinha, 2012).

The use and generation of theory by inclusive researchers is interesting and one of the focuses for reflection and dialogue among inclusive researchers in the learning disability field (Nind and Vinha, 2012). Bjornsdottir and Svensdottir (2008) use Bourdieu's (1984) theory of social capital to explore a conundrum. People with learning disabilities, they argue, have little cultural capital in the field of disability studies where there is a need to use scholarly language to compete for power and 'maximise profit by following the rules set by the dominant group' (p. 268). Simultaneously, non-disabled supporters/allies also lack capital in the field of disability studies by dint of not being disabled. They therefore see writing the academic paper as a collaboration in which they are 'gambling for capital'.

Gay and Grey – PAR in the context of a complex collaboration

The Gay and Grey project is another complex collaboration in research, this time a 'joint initiative between a voluntary agency working with older people' and a university (Fenge, 2010, pp. 881–2). It shows how people can work together across difference for common (and some individual) good. The research, funded by the Big Lottery, was aimed at identifying factors and issues contributing towards the exclusion of gay people from the wider community of older people and from support services, and at identifying how to address these to promote greater social inclusion. Fenge (2010) argues that the collaborative approach was born from a context of increasing policy and practice emphasis on working in partnership. It was motivated by a desire to get unheard voices heard, to be anti-oppressive and to value diversity. The university and voluntary agency partners chose

PAR as their approach as they were not older/lesbians themselves and they were acutely aware, therefore, of their problematic status as outsiders. They addressed this by recruiting 'volunteer' insiders, thereby securing user involvement for the pilot work and at the stage of securing funding. Once the volunteers were recruited they were able to negotiate the aims of the project and a commitment to participatory approach.

While Fenge, the academic, has written about the process and the politics of the inclusive research, many of the products of this research that relate to the substantive findings are collaboratively written with the 'volunteers' (another new term to describe the lay people involved) who were active in dissemination as they were in all stages of the work. Fenge (2010) reflects on the principles (from Whitmore and McGee, 2001, p. 396) that governed their way of working together: non-intrusive collaboration, mutual trust and respect, solidarity, mutuality and equality, a focus on process, and language as an expression of culture and power. She is honest about the volunteers having different aims and motivations from the university and voluntary agency partners, but she recognizes that this is usual in PAR. The 'outsider' researchers were more pressured by the funder requirements and the volunteers were keener to rush to action. She also relates some of the divisions of labour that arose, with women ending up leading the research part and men doing the outreach work; she regrets that without people from minority ethnic communities being involved there was still an element of silencing of some. Interestingly, we see that among the different aspirations and roles of the volunteers, and with some ebb and flow of personnel, a small group emerged as the most comfortable with mutual learning and became what Fenge (2010, p. 886) refers to as 'co-learners' – those with whom there was a strong feeling of solidarity and long-lived collaboration. For Fenge (2010), crucial elements in the success of this inclusive research were the central role played by dialogue and the time needed for trust to develop (for which the funding to permit this was essential). The pattern that emerges repeatedly is that inclusive research takes time, and the additional time is not just for the business of making the relationships work (Byrne et al., 2009; Nind and Vinha, 2012; Lewis and MacLeod, in press).

Hearing (our) voices – PAR in a contrasting context

Another example of inclusive research using the PAR approach, a collaboration between an academic and lay people diagnosed with schizophrenia, comes from Calgary, Canada and is narrated in detail by Schneider (2010) (the draft having been considered by the wider group). This example is useful because of the detail and the passion in the account. Schneider and the Unsung Heroes Peer Support Group undertook two pieces of inclusive research together: one small project about communication between people diagnosed with schizophrenia and their medical professionals, and one larger research project about housing for people diagnosed with schizophrenia. The first project was prompted by a funding call that led to the academic making contact with the group and their developing a proposal together. The second project arose from concerns raised by group members as well as a desire to do further research. In both cases the academic (who was also the mother of a young adult with schizophrenia) was instrumental in seeing the funding opportunities, but these were not studies led by the academic or the support group: they were studies planned, conducted and disseminated together. As Schneider (2010, pp. 31–2) sums up:

> Our projects fall somewhere between collaboration and control. I initiated the first project, but the research group members initiated the second and in both projects they had a significant degree of control over decision-making in all aspects of the research and dissemination. I became the facilitator, trainer, and supporter rather than the expert researcher, providing the information they needed to make decisions, but not making the decisions for them. . . . We negotiated ways to accomplish their goals without compromising the progress of the research.

The dissemination included a co-written academic paper, theatre productions, documentary film and poster book.

In introducing the book about the research Schneider (2010, pp. 13–14) stresses features of PAR that were important to them: democratic process, co-operative inquiry with co-researchers, using the expertise of lived experience, transforming 'the social relations of research by regarding participants as both co-researchers and co-subjects', with 'an emancipatory or empowerment agenda'. She argues that 'as participatory research is fundamentally about "the right to speak" it offers people diagnosed with schizophrenia a way to both reclaim a positive identity and make a contribution to society' (p. 35). These ideas and premises are recurrent themes throughout this book. The research, drawing on Fisher (1984), adds the dimension of narrative as a way of knowing and as a basis of community. This element of sharing stories and ultimately creating a common story is implicit rather than explicit in many of the accounts of inclusive research. It is important as a means for validating different voices, narratives and narrators.

Schneider (2010) is an advocate for many of the ideas included in Chapter 2 as the drivers and influences on the evolution of inclusive research practices. For example, she makes the case for the useful, unique and superior knowledge that inclusive research can generate:

> Inclusion of people diagnosed with schizophrenia in all aspects of knowledge production about schizophrenia, that is, in research, has the potential to produce knowledge that is not available in any other way. People with schizophrenia themselves know best about their experiences and what helps them to cope with these experiences. They are able to steer the research to the issues and concerns that are most important to them. Focusing the research in this way has the potential to provide information that can dramatically improve the care that people diagnosed with schizophrenia receive. (p. 25)

The claims she makes are tempered by phrasing about 'potential', indicating that these advantages are possible rather than automatic. Nonetheless, while these kinds of claims are harder to see in practice in some domains, they are evidenced in Schneider's (2010) book. One thing that helped in the democratization of expertise was that, as the academic, she was not an expert in mental health and so may have felt less the temptation for her knowledge to trump that of the co-researchers; instead, the necessary expertise was held very much among themselves as a team. Another claim relates to the aspiration for inclusive research to 'give voice' to marginalized people. Schneider (2010) is not alone in making the case for this and also in grappling with the dynamic of not being bossy or dominating (see Nind and Vinha, 2012). The research findings, though, testify to the value of partnership in decision making achieved through 'open and collegial communication' (p. 25) and to the impact benefits of public voice achieved through active involvement in dissemination.

An issue for inclusive research is that it is often set up to perform multiple roles in multiple ways. A key concern that has arisen for me in researching inclusive research is whether we ask too much of it (Nind and Vinha, 2012, 2013). For example, the research is meant to produce valid, even superior knowledge, and at the same time produce tangible training, networking, social and employment benefits for those involved. Schneider (2010, p. 26) considers this and concludes that 'the benefits we experienced [particularly overcoming isolation and gaining a sense of connection] are as important as the knowledge we produced, although they are a welcome by-product rather than a direct goal of the projects'. This position may reflect her role as narrator of the research story and her preoccupations as an academic researcher and grant-holder. Nonetheless, the range of benefits and their power emerge strongly from her account.

Academic-led research

Some argue that academic-led research, by its very nature, cannot be termed inclusive research in any meaningful sense. However, academic-led research includes rich accounts of how an inclusive research process may work in practice. MacLeod et al. (2013) comment that the detail of participatory methods is more often underreported, making it difficult to know what it is that researchers do that effectively enhances the active participation of their participants in parts or the whole of the process. These more transparent accounts, therefore, are all the more valuable.

The use of participatory methods in qualitative research – giving children choice

I begin the section on academic-led research with an example that epitomizes the kinds of moves that academics make to be participatory. Many academic researchers design their studies, or at least their methods, to maximize the active engagement of participants. This may be considered participatory research or research using participatory methods. The extent to which it is inclusive research, or differs from other forms of qualitative research, is contested (see Chapter 4). It is important to examine the dynamic between the researcher and the researched, who do not become merged or transformed in this kind of inclusive research but do come closer together with potential for reciprocity. Much of this research is with children and young people. Thomas and O'Kane (1998) discuss the process of their research about children's participation in decision making when they are looked after by local authorities. They initially designed their research and set their objectives then began setting about maximizing the participation of their child participants. They explain: 'we would claim that the conduct of the research was participatory in a stronger sense than merely that it employed "user-friendly" materials; children were involved not only in choosing how they participated personally but in consciously influencing the direction of the research and in making decisions about its dissemination' (p. 341). This concept of children choosing is fundamental to their approach, providing children with a choice of activities which included answering questions among other flexible and creative options. Thus children could opt to be involved in techniques that were more or less verbal or visual in orientation, and adapted to their individual preferences.

Thomas and O'Kane (1998) were acting on their view of the social child as agent and drawing ideas from life story work/PRA to offer data collection activities such as timelines, 'my favourite place', and 'what I would change with my magic wand' (p. 343). Their desire for children to have an active role in the research included a concern with the analysis stages. The first part of this involved the children being able to 'choose subjects for discussion and decide what they wanted to say about them' and extended into following 'their understanding of questions and concepts as well as ours' (p. 345). Secondly, there was an element of returning to the children more than once to provide the opportunity for them to review and refine their data. Thirdly, they describe 'using group processes' thereby creating 'space where children could collectively reinterpret the research questions and do further work on the material brought from the individual interviews' (p. 345). They thus ended up with a strong sense of the co-construction of knowledge:

> Finally, at the conclusion of the research we worked with a group of eight volunteers from among the 47 children to make an audiotape of children's comments from the research. This involved the group in helping to select and edit the comments in order to get across the messages which we and they agreed should be taken from the research. Throughout this process our own understanding of what were the important questions and the critical evidence concerning children's participation in decisions developed reflexively with the children's successive contributions to the research process. In the end it is hard to disentangle what was our contribution and what was theirs; but there is no doubt that the course followed by the research, and the final conclusions, were very different as a result of the children's own interpretations of the data. (p. 345)

Choice and voice – when anything other than academic-led research seems impossible

Some contexts allow choice even when they do not lend themselves to partnership or lay researcher-led research. For example, Conolly (2008, p. 208) found that the 'full' participatory research she aspired to in her research with excluded school girls was unfeasible as their own difficult lives presented barriers to them bringing the commitment and ethical care needed. Nonetheless, Conolly still wanted them to enjoy 'some ownership of the research process', and so she adopted 'the middle ground' of 'seeking to understand their lives and what was important to them' by using 'the reflexive co-construction of biographies through task-based interviewing' (p. 208). This involved plenty of choice and an exchange of information as she herself joined in the process of sharing.

In a similar action-oriented study, colleagues and I engaged with girls excluded from mainstream school and their new special school staff and we looked to give the girls choice from a range of verbal and visual methods (Clarke et al., 2011). The research was aimed at developing an evidence-based holistic curriculum model for girls with behavioural, social and emotional difficulties. How the girls experienced various curricula and schools was as important to us as the academic evidence. We were acutely aware that, for such girls who contravene social and gender norms and become marginalized in their social status, the opportunities to have their voices heard and views trusted are sparse; there is no self-advocacy movement among troubled youngsters and individual attempts to speak out are interpreted through the lens of the young person being troublesome. We were also aware, as Charmaz (2008, p. 14) powerfully argues, that being on the margins 'offers fresh interpretations of the centre, and may open possibilities for renewal, change and transformation'. While we appreciated Greene's (2009) warning that being asked to participate in research activities can feel like yet another adult-initiated chore, we were also convinced by Holland et al.'s (2008) argument that we could avoid this adult-centredness by enabling young people to choose how they communicated with us. Policy shifts towards hearing pupils' voices had led to somewhat superficial processes around this so we expected the girls were likely to be cynical unless we offered genuine choices. We did not perceive a simple process of giving the girls voice but, rather, influenced by Alcoff's (1992) *The Problem of Speaking for Others*, sought to engage with the girls' voices, sensitive to our own privileged position and to the socio-political context. We were not seeking to silence ourselves or others, but to facilitate imaginative listening (Corbett, 1998) and transformative dialogue (Fielding, 2004).

The operationalization of our aspirations and critically nuanced understandings of voice involved enabling the girls to draw on their preferences and competences as communicators. It also involved us developing our capacity as listeners. We sought to establish that we were all taking risks, within some safe boundaries, and that we were creating spaces for meaningful communication. This was not in the shape of anything the girls might interpret as counselling or imposing; rather, we offered opportunities to use the range of digital media available in the school's strongly visual environment. This extended to the consent process in which some of the girls helped to develop comic-strip style information sheets, developing their understanding of the issues while personalizing them and making them visual.

There was one particular method among an array offered that the girls took real ownership of – the video diary. The diary room, partly attractive because of the television series *Big Brother*, became a space they customized and made good use of. It suited them, with some girls going in independently and spontaneously to speak to camera and some preferring to speak with adults present or to be called to talk about a specific topic. In the diary room they felt safe and supported to reflect and did so readily, providing graphic accounts of school experiences in which their voices had not been sought or heard and of sense of disconnection from school. Their narratives highlighted the importance to them of student-centred systems for listening at the heart of the curriculum to represent that staff are open and care.

This project, while far from being participatory throughout the design and whole process, genuinely valued the girls' participation as active co-constructors of an understanding of how the curriculum should be designed. We found that 'the girls communicated openly, insightfully and, at times, at length with regard to a number of features relating to access to their schooling' (Clarke et al., 2011, p. 776). The option to participate as they wished enabled this to happen; furthermore, it facilitated the girls being viewed differently by the staff and by themselves. This did little to disrupt the asymmetric power relations of schooling, but it did disrupt some privileging and silencing of voices and it did generate worthwhile insights and fresh narratives.

Overcoming barriers to participation: Researching with adults on the autistic spectrum

Turning to a different participant group, academics have sought to overcome barriers to the participation in research of young adults on the autistic spectrum by working with the participants themselves to address the barriers and effective methods. MacLeod et al. (2013) argue that the social and communication difficulties of people with autism, and the perceptions of others around these, have a profound impact on their opportunities for inclusion in research. They observe that it is 'difficult and risky for "outsider" researchers to second guess the motivations and interpretations of individuals who may view the world very differently'. This is beginning to be corroborated, they suggest, by 'a small but growing body of evidence suggesting that research consulting directly with autistic participants can reveal findings to challenge current understandings' and that the insights generated show the value on more nuanced 'insider' perspectives. Yet the application of participatory approaches with individuals with autism is still very new and researchers are focusing on how this can be achieved.

MacLeod et al. (2013) reflect on their methodology in a study involving ten higher education students diagnosed as being on the autism spectrum, using interpretative phenomenological analysis to privilege the participants' expertise on their own experience. A pilot phase led to the identification of potential barriers to participation including participants' anxieties about the communication and interview process, time management challenges and potential for miscommunication. Again, providing choice for participants was the primary approach for addressing these and participants were able to choose between face-to-face, telephone or synchronous (real-time) online interview (although, against expectations, face-to-face was most preferred). Making the interview as predictable as possible was also important and participants were able to prepare in advance using a prompt sheet sent to them to help them identify significant events for educational success as a common frame of reference in interviews. There was also a comprehensive system of reminders that was valued by participants.

The research involved some negotiation around voice. A structured process of respondent validation involved transcript checking and dialogue about the researchers' initial analysis. The researchers were explicit that in the case of different interpretations both would be reported. Their findings illustrate the ways in which participants engaged with honesty and commitment in the process of analysis. It was through these follow-up dia-logues about the interpretation of data that 'the spaces between autistic and non-autistic interpretations could be explored and common ground identified' (MacLeod et al., 2013). The authors reflect on how much time was involved in conducting research that accommodated the needs of the autistic participants, which was possible given that they were working outside of the constraints of an externally funded project and timeline. They also reflect on the motivation of participants to be involved in research that might benefit others with autism (thus challenging notions of a lack of empathy being inherent to the condition). The research was perceived 'by its end-users as important and relevant to them' (MacLeod et al., 2013), perhaps to some extent as empowering for them. Seeing the research process from the participants' perspective is important and these researchers conclude that this means getting the balance of demands and commitment right for participants, rather than in accord with one's own assumptions or aspirations as researchers. Here they echo Bourke (2009), who observes that her participants did not always agree with the premise of 'the more participatory the better'.

An organic approach to involving children and young people

Next I contrast the more managed examples with some in which the nature of the participation evolves more organically. In the earlier exam-ples the academic narrators are at pains to emphasize the ethical, flexible and responsive nature of their methodological approach, yet the children and young people were not able to shape the actual research questions. In their *(Extra)ordinary Lives* study, Holland et al. (2008) used an ethno-graphic approach to conduct research with children and young people and, simultaneously, to study their participatory research processes. In adopting this approach they limited the extent to which, as academic researchers, they predetermined their focus.

Holland et al. (2008, p. 11) regard some participatory research as 'more managed' compared to their 'less directive' and 'organic' approach. They used some formal participatory techniques, but found that these 'were less successful at generating data than more free-flowing, unplanned data generation techniques that mimicked more closely the young people's everyday means of communication' (p. 13). Moreover, they saw data analy-sis as integral rather than a separate stage and so their children and young people were involved in analysis through their 'informal interactions seeking feedback'; this was ongoing rather than bounded. The authors reflect on how always sharing the emerging findings with the children and young people enhanced transparency but did not necessarily deepen understanding around those findings. From their experience they conclude:

> We would argue that it is more important to pay close attention to *how* participation is enacted (at a range of levels, including participant-participant, participant-researchers, groups of participants-groups of workers, participants-end-users of research, including policy makers and academic audiences) than to focus in on *how much* participation was achieved. Meaningful exchanges, where individuals and groups have choices in what they wish to share, with whom and in what way, would seem to be at least as important as ensuring that participatory mechanisms are in place, such as advisory groups. Ticking participatory boxes, in civic participation practice or in research does not necessarily mean that participants experience the process as participatory, nor will it always affect the outcomes. (pp. 24–5)

Academics sometimes need to launch a project and allow this organic development for participation to grow.

Examples of academics engaging in dialogue

My next examples are important for the stress the researchers place on dialogue between themselves and participants. Participants may experience research in terms of being explicitly engaged in particular events or processes, or they may have the experience of being engaged in genuine dialogue with the academic researcher. This is one approach to increasing participants' agency in research that doctoral researchers whom I have supervised have made meaningful. Vinha (2011) made a conscious decision to make dialogue central to her research design about children's identities and experiences. This was rooted in the ideas of Freire (1967, 1970) and the idea of *conscientização*, that is, the act of ordinary or oppressed people coming to know the social, political and economic context of injustices and consequently taking action against the oppressive components of that given reality involving simultaneous reflection and action. Freire (1970, p. 27) was clear that any empowerment of oppressed people needed to be done by and for themselves. He asks, 'who are better prepared than the oppressed to understand the terrible significance of an oppressed society? Who suffer the effects of oppression more than the oppressed? Who can better understand the necessity of liberation?' Freire regards dialogue as playing a key role in this empowerment as without it people's 'perception of themselves as oppressed is impaired by their submersion in the reality of oppression' (p. 27).

Vinha, in turn, set out to make the process of generating narrative through open-ended interviews into a dialogue, and to make it inclusive by adopting a radical position of solidarity with her participants. Her dialogical method of inquiry involved (1) listening to all voices, (2) 'a reflective process which embraces the praxis of naming the world collaboratively' and (3) methods to address power imbalances between the researcher and researched embedded in the social process. She worked with Freire's premises that dialogue requires humility, hope and critical thinking to develop the idea of a cyclical dialogic inquiry process. The starting point in this process is 'the researcher's humility and faith in the participants' capability to actively contribute to the research' and their 'openness to the participants as the basis of the dialogue' (Vinha, 2011, p. 86). There then follows a series of encounters, each involving an interview and follow-up consultation to hear each participant's own interpretation of what they have said and done so that sense-making is collaborative. Periods of reflection would then guide the next step in the interview-consultation-reflection cycle with the participant-researchers/ researcher-participants (the terminology Vinha chooses to reflect the duality of their roles).

Vinha (2011) also wanted to act on the concept of Clough and Barton (1998, p. 129) of turning up the volume on participants' (possibly timid) voices in her writing. Using narrative to organize experience also involved telling the dynamics as well as the content of the dialogue. To these ends she experimented with both verbal voice and visual voice as complementary to each other in the processes of forming the dialogue and telling the research story. Findings were presented in a relatively straightforward literal telling and through a more fictional/metaphorical account, though she asserts that neither is more truthful or authentic. The latter though was used to represent the findings in a more accessible, engaging and enabling way. It also enabled her to be more honest about some of the power struggles with the adults who she had hoped would facilitate in her dialogue with the children.

Sherwood (2011) placed a similar emphasis on dialogue in her research exploring how parents of young disabled children experienced support. For her, the dialogue came through optimizing her abilities to listen to and attune to the parent-participants and through turning their opportunities to comment on transcripts and other data into conversations. She refers to the process as 'reciprocal meaning-making' in the quest to retain the 'integrity and authenticity of their story and mine' (p. 89). Sherwood's work shows how concerns to use ethnographic case study type approaches to represent insiders' views is at the juncture between everyday qualitative research and inclusive research. The latter comes through in her emphasis on participatory dialogue and reciprocity, her desire to subject her own and her participants' perspectives to challenge in a transactional process in which they might change each other, and in the way in which their stories become intertwined.

The Mosaic approach – description of a method for use with young children

In the next example, the idea of dialogue is expanded to include layers of participants. Here the ideas of Holland et al. (2008) about how the participants experience their participation, and the role of dialogue in inclusive research, have resonance in Clark's (2001) description of the Mosaic approach. This is an approach designed to maximize the involvement of very young children in research about the learning environments that are best suited to them. The Mosaic approach, more codified than organic, is led by the adults in the formal research role but carefully designed to avoid tokenism.

Stage one involves gathering data through observation, child conferencing (a form of interview), using cameras and photos as an alternative language, tours and mapping of the environment, guided walks to get 'local knowledge', and seeking parents' and practitioners' comments. Stage two involves 'piecing together the Mosaic for dialogue, reflection and interpretation' (Clark, 2001, p. 338) in a process of meaning making. This process is carried out through discussion among children, practitioners and researchers – in different combinations and forms. It can involve preverbal children in which case there is more emphasis on observation, attuning to body language, and observations by siblings/other children. Clark (2001) is explicit about the outcomes of Stage two. For children the product is a 'tangible portrait of their experiences', such as photographs, which are a 'source of pride' together with increased skills and confidence plus a 'chance to reflect' and to raise concerns (p. 339). For practitioners and parents, 'using the Mosaic approach makes the children's experiences accessible to parents in a new way' (p. 340). In addition, practitioners and parents can also 'express their perspectives and gain in confidence' (p. 340). At an institutional level the outcome is a change in culture. The whole process cultivates a 'culture of listening', which means children develop understanding, collaboration is supported and mutual respect is established. Clark contrasts this with a 'culture of measurement', in which 'consulting children aims to extract their preformed views, listening is for adults' agendas only, and practitioners' views are absent in the discussions which follow' (p. 340).

The Mosaic approach is regarded as an inclusive approach with some integrity. It differs from child-led research in that adults play a vital role, but it is strongly guided by a concern with children's agendas and perspectives and by a concept of their competence to hold and share vital knowledge. It is very much about knowledge construction rather than extraction. It positions children as experts, skilful communicators, active participants and meaning makers, researchers and explorers (Todd, 2012) alongside the academic researchers.

Steering groups

Another codified approach to dialogue is the use of steering groups and this is often favoured by funding bodies. The commissioners of the research are, after all, a complicated part of the researcher–researched relationship (Sin and Fong, 2010) and have their own ideas and parameters. In dialogue with inclusive researchers working in diverse ways in the field of learning disability research, it became apparent that one of the features distinguishing academic-led research from lay researcher-led research or partnership research was who funded the research (Nind and Vinha, 2012). Two research funders, Joseph Rowntree Foundation and Heritage Lottery Fund, were particularly attuned to the idea of adults with learning disabilities leading research into their own lives or histories and valued the social inclusion benefits as well as the knowledge benefits gained by carrying out research this way.

More commonly, bodies commissioning research have favoured research led by academics. For example, bodies commissioning research about the experiences of disabled children, such as the Disability Rights Commission, have slightly different agendas from the Joseph Rowntree Foundation and Heritage Lottery Fund about ensuring that children's voices are heard. 'It behoves us to recognize that aspirations and expectations for, and experiences of, "hearing" from disabled children and young people unfold as a delicate balancing act where different agendas are at work, and where different rights and authority levels are negotiated oftentimes implicitly' (Sin and Fong, 2010, pp. 18–19). Hearing disabled children's voices via funded research has tended to be trusted to academics rather than to disabled adults or to children themselves. This does not mean that those academics have not strived to be authentic in their response to the challenge.

One option favoured by some research funders for making academic-led research more inclusive is the use of reference or advisory groups. Lewis et al. (2008) reflected on the use of such groups in relation to three projects. Lewis et al. (2007) were funded by the Disability Rights Commission to research the experiences of disabled pupils and their families with the aim of identifying the pupils' and families' key concerns and priorities related to education. This involved a reference group of two highly involved disabled people and advisory committees of disabled people. These committees were bigger and less involved than the reference group, but they were already established before the research began. Watson et al. (2007) were funded by the Esmee Fairbairn Foundation to explore approaches by which disabled children with little or no verbal communication could be included in educational decision making. They involved an established reference group of young disabled people – the Listening Partnership – as well as a conventional advisory committee of academics, professionals and parents. In the third project, the Foundation for People with Learning Disabilities and researchers from the University of Cambridge (Byers et al., 2008) were funded by the Big Lottery Fund to conduct PAR with young people with learning difficulties. The aim was to improve the young people's experience through better educational inclusion in mainstream schools and colleges. This project involved support from an advisory committee of professionals, policy makers and parents, and from a reference group of young people from Speaking Up, a local advocacy, training and consultancy organization for young people with learning difficulties. Lewis et al. (2008) reflected on this arrangement, and highlighted the need for care planning for the involvement of advisory group members (including matters of payment). Lewis et al. also reflected that creating, extending or capitalizing on an existing group to advise projects is valuable, especially when there is a good skills match but the group is not overprofessionalized. Nonetheless, they conclude: 'While there is powerful rhetoric surrounding such work [with reference groups], progress will only be made if honest and transparent accounts highlight the possible complexities and tensions alongside the undoubted benefits' (p. 82).

Urbanfields – the use of participatory video within research

My final example is participatory video, a visual and action-oriented approach that offers a different way of incorporating marginalized voices in research increasingly used by NGOs and fostering deeper engagement with communities. Those particularly interested should also explore this under the labels of participatory film making or community or collaborative video. A specific example comes from Haw and Hadfield (2011) who describe altogether different challenges and solutions to those discussed earlier in their research about the risk repertoires of young people living in 'Urbanfields', an area known for gang and drug culture: 'Our research involved working with these young people on quite sensitive subjects, and so video was seen as a means of accessing their views, without "frightening off" participants through intrusive personal questioning' (p. 100). Their video was not in the form of video diaries as Clarke, Boorman and I used, but culminated in 'two trigger films, six films made by the young people themselves and a final DVD created by the research team' (p. 100). The first trigger video made to recruit participants was shown in the local community centre after extensive leafleting. It was designed to provoke interest by showing the different ways that different groups including professional and media perceive the young people and the risks they take. It challenged the local young people to consider how they would want to portray themselves. It captured and juxtaposed different views alongside the very familiar images of the local area that were needed to prompt recognition and engage interest. Crucial to achieving this, and crucial to the overall study, was the involvement of community-based researchers known within the community who were able to provide an 'insider's view' (p. 102).

In this project six different groups (reflecting differences in dominant ethnic group, gender and age) negotiated the focus of a video they would make to represent their lives, to be owned and used by them. The academic researchers facilitated and researched the video making process, filming it to provide another layer of data for analysis. In a subsequent phase the researchers' footage was edited with the original trigger video to focus on themes important to the young people and shown as a trigger video to new groups of professionals and young people to elicit responses in focus group and individual interviews. Thus the myths around the local cultures were exposed and reflected upon at different stages and multiple interpretations were explored. Haw and Hadfield (2011, pp. 103–4) reflect on the participants' agency throughout:

> As the participants made numerous decisions about the content of their videos, their 'internal narratives', spaces for critical subjectivity, were opened up, reflecting their broader agency. Crucially though, as these videos were produced and shown to different audiences, the potential to enhance this reflexivity and criticality was developed. ... Getting participants to engage with collectively held myths ... in their own videos involved incorporating elements, within the video process, of what they considered ordinary and everyday within their locality with what was perceived as extraordinary by those outside it, and exploring why this was so. An exploration of these mythologies relied on the collective experience of the participants and professionals. In this way, the internal and external narratives of the different videos revealed through the production and consumption processes also highlighted the connections between the 'felt' worlds of the participants and how they then fed these back into wider social discourses operating around them.

Learning the art of inclusive research

The examples in this chapter illustrate the range of approaches, methods and skills employed by researchers seeking to conduct their research inclusively in some way. Some of the examples show researchers learning in a formal way about the rules of engagement of research. This may be people new to research, such as children, learning traditional research methods, or people familiar to research, such as academics, learning new ways of relating to and including others (and much in between). Some of the examples show researchers learning though doing, usually from and within the dynamic research teams they have formed, in a kind of apprenticeship or knowledge exchange model. Rarely have the research teams been trained to do research inclusively as such.

Learning through doing is not always straightforward, and Smith (2012, p. 11) recounts indigenous researchers learning through doing who 'get hurt and fail in the process'. In a different context, but addressing similar issues, Warren and Boxall (2009) recognized the lack of training for people wanting to do research in partnerships spanning academics and service users in the field of social work. They therefore describe the rationale for, and development of, their Researching Together short course. This brought different groups together to learn from and with each other and to 'raise questions about the "us" and "them" of learning, teaching and research as well as about the idea of "expert knowledge"' (p. 287). The course was prompted by government pushes for service user involvement in social work research as well as policy and practice, and by the authors' concerns 'about the exclusion of many service users, particularly those viewed as "less articulate", from these arenas'. The course created opportunities for undergraduates 'to get to know, share space, communicate with, work alongside, and be challenged by service users', not least because it 'was set up in such a way that the knowledges and experiences of service users were prioritised over the research literature and academic theory which underpins most social policy courses'. This was a conscious alternative to 'objectifying' service users (p. 288), which happens when their knowledge is tacked on rather than embedded in research learning. They used Harding's (2004) idea that dominant groups are 'epistemologically disadvantaged' when trying to research non-dominant groups and their experiences (p. 289).

The Researching Together training is unusual in the way that it positions and handles expertise. Warren and Boxall are not alone, however, in recognizing that training is needed. Courses (particularly postgraduate) are emerging in which there is a focus on inclusive, participatory and emancipatory approaches to working and researching. Some of these (e.g. the Norah Fry Research Centre, University of Bristol and Critical Learning Disability Studies, University of Manchester) feature involvement in lecturing by 'experts by experience', thus further blurring the boundaries between academic and lay researchers and teachers. Similarly materials are being developed to support researchers wanting to do research inclusively (see Further reading and resources).

There is much to be learned by inclusive researchers reflecting on their practices and disseminating information about their processes as well as findings. However, this is dependent on the quality of engagement in critical reflection. Sin and Fong (2010, p. 21) argue that: 'Meaningful and successful involvement will always be a journey of learning, to be approached with humility and conviction.' Walmsley and Johnson (2003, p. 2) make a strong case that, in the field of learning disability, researchers have stood back from this challenge of critical reflection somewhat, owing to the sensitivity of issues, leading to a 'certain stifling of debate about the real difficulties of including people with learning disabilities in research'. They have called for 'certain orthodoxies and assumptions' to be challenged 'in order to clarify what inclusive research is and how and where it can be applied'. Grant and Ramcharan (2007, p. 12) have similarly called for those involved in inclusive research to reflect on their experience and on 'what forms of partnership make inclusive research effective, and whether good science and good inclusive research practice can be brought together'.

Doing Research Inclusively, Doing Research Well? (Nind and Vinha, 2012) was in part a response to the call for collective reflection and to what Walmsley and Johnson (2003, p. 16) identified as a 'failure to grapple honestly' with the most sensitive questions. In this study, more than 60 researchers entered into dialogue in focus groups. Recurrent narratives emerged about working in partnership, listening to and learning from each other. Participant-researchers particularly stressed the importance of enabling new researchers by making things accessible, checking things out with them and being honest. From analysis of the transcripts we were able to generate a model (see Figure 3.1) that represents the options for co-researching.

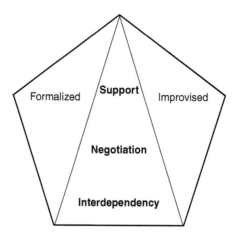

Figure 3.1 Model of working together practices in inclusive research.

Formalized approaches include working with preplanned rules or formal reference groups while improvised (or responsive) approaches are worked out in the doing – responding to challenges as they emerge. Some research teams did both within the same project. Ways of working that emphasized support reflected an inherent assumption that there were experts and non-experts – leaders and supporters – although the basis for the expertise could vary. Supporters would subdue their urges to speak or make decisions, not seeing this as their role. As one supporter (Karen) explained, 'It's not always easy, because I may have an opinion . . . but I think that ultimately we make sure the co-researchers make the decisions' (Nind and Vinha, 2013, p. 5). Ways of working that emphasized negotiation involved considerable time and energy spent negotiating practices and principles for practice before any research could happen. This was sometimes as important to the people involved as the research itself, reflecting their desire to distance themselves from past wrongs or traditional research processes. Ways of working that emphasized interdependency still valued support and negotiation, but these were secondary to co-operation in teamwork involving high levels of trust and communication. Research challenges could be tackled collectively or by allocating roles and tasks according to people's different strengths. Interdependence came from no-one being regarded as more expert than any other, such that they did not need the other. While the model may be helpful it simplifies diverse practices. These were not fixed according to any one dimension of the model and evolved with greater involvement, critical turning points, exposure to new ideas, or learning from mistakes.

Doing Research Inclusively, Doing Research Well? (Nind and Vinha, 2012) generated various materials intended to support researchers wanting to work in inclusive ways including a prompt sheet of questions designed to provoke reflection and discussion rather than suggest that there is one right way. The questions are listed in Table 3.1.

The research demonstrated the ways in which inclusive researchers are still learning their craft, using the limited possibilities for funded research to enact principled positions as far as practicable. We concluded therefore that 'it must surely be too early to fix and pin down too tightly the research approach that we call inclusive research' (Nind and Vinha, 2013, p. 7). Rather than inclusive research 'becoming the new "normality"', we argued that 'an expansive vision of inclusive research is necessary for its sustainability' (p. 7). In the next chapter I discuss some of the threats to inclusive research and some of the criticisms made of the concepts and practices.

Table 3.1 Questions to ask yourself when working out how to work together in inclusive research

1	Why are you working together on the research? Do you have a shared purpose, or do you want different things from it?
2	What do you each understand inclusive research to be?
3	What values guide the way you want to work together? How will you put those values into action?
4	What terms will you use to describe yourselves (co-researchers, partners, team members, etc.)? What does your choice of the terms say about you?
5	How will you talk about the research? (How often, where, etc.)
6	Who is setting the agenda?
7	Does everyone have equal right to speak? How will you make sure everyone is heard?
8	What skills, knowledge and qualities do each of you offer?
9	What will you do together and what tasks will you need to divide out?
10	What can you plan in advance and where might you need to adapt as you go along?
11	What kinds of support are needed?
12	How will you work through differences of opinion and challenges?
13	How will you learn from each other?
14	Are you placing most importance on support, on negotiation or on interdependence?
15	What will work best for this particular project at this time?

4 Inclusive research under fire: Criticisms and defences

In Chapters 1 and 2, I described some of the claims and distinguishing features of inclusive research. In Chapter 3, I expanded on the nature of inclusive research using examples. I have also pointed out the concern that the detail of how the research is conducted inclusively is often omitted from research reporting and that the challenges of conducting it are inadequately confronted and reflected upon. In this chapter I turn much more to this and other criticisms of inclusive research. These criticisms arise, in part, from claims made for the kinds of research said to be inclusive, participatory or emancipatory. Frankham (2009, p. 16), for example, points out, 'there is a tendency in this field to over-claim the benefits of partnership working and to avoid acknowledging the complexities of the field'. She also points to the need to counter the 'celebratory narrative[s]' without necessarily undermining 'the idea or the ideal of carrying out research with service users'. Like Frankham (2009), Walmsley and Johnson (2003) and others, I regard raising and debating key questions about inclusive research as important to its development, as well as important to extending understanding of what is inclusive research. It is unhelpful for this field of research to be closed to criticism. Instead, in this chapter I follow Frankham's lead in taking seriously the encouragement from Lather (1991) 'to trouble notions of service user involvement from a concern that: "narratives of salvage and redemptive agendas can be ever deeper places for privilege to hide"' (p. 16). I organize the critique of research in relation to the claims made for it. Thus, I discuss in turn the critical debates surrounding the claims that:

1. inclusive research leads to more authentic/better knowledge,
2. inclusive research is more ethical,
3. inclusive research addresses the power imbalances between researcher and researched,
4. inclusive research is inclusive of people who have been silenced by traditional research,

5. inclusive research, particularly emancipatory research, is empowering,
6. inclusive research solves problems; it is a panacea for many research ills.

Inclusive research leads to more authentic/better knowledge

The claim that inclusive research leads to more authentic and therefore better knowledge relates to one of the core ideas underpinning inclusive research discussed in Chapter 2. The claim for authenticity rests on knowledge being grounded in the experiences and values of those concerned. Service users/children – or whoever – turned researchers/co-researchers – or whatever term is used – are considered expert on matters concerning them, privileged in inclusive research terms as insiders. This is the basis for claiming that knowledge produced by them, or resulting from pursuing questions identified by them, is more valid. It is also the basis for claiming inclusive research contributes to more valid, more holistic knowledge, not least because it has previously been missing from the dominant picture.

The critical debate around this claim arises from questioning whether insider knowledge is necessarily more accurate or authentic. Such questioning can be about resisting the temptation to somehow reify those with minority status. James (2007, cited by Porter et al., 2012) raises this question in relation to children's research. Policy- or decision makers may not trust the rigour of young people's research. There may be tensions between accepting children's analysis and accepting analysis that locates findings in the wider context and aids theory building (Coad and Evans, 2008). Nonetheless, Todd (2012) notes that within inclusive research children's voices are often treated and regarded uncritically.

Gallacher and Gallagher (2008, p. 499) go further in their concerns with the 'increasing dominance of "participatory" approaches and uncritical ways in which they are often deployed'. For them much of the superiority of participatory approaches is about appearance: appearing emancipatory and democratic or seeming to have 'an epistemological advantage over more traditional approaches' (p. 499). They build on critiques of participatory methods emerging in development studies and human geography and they question the basic epistemological premise that we are best placed to know ourselves and people like us, that 'people are transparently knowable to themselves' and therefore the 'most authentic source of knowledge about themselves and their lives' (p. 501). This argument is of fundamental importance as it gets to the very heart of inclusive research.

Some inclusive researchers already work from the premise that people may not know themselves best, but they do know themselves differently. This gives rise to the stance that the narratives of lay researchers or participants are *as* important, but not necessarily *more* important than those of traditional researchers. This can fit with the critique of Gallacher and Gallagher (2008), who do not hold academic researchers as experts either, instead arguing that we are all interdependent – all methodologically immature – and therefore all with potential. The pluralist compromise is that for authentic knowledge we need to bring together knowledges 'from diverse actors within different generations [or situations] and so ensure that maximum benefits accrue' (Porter et al., 2012, p. 132). Questions about privileging certain knowledge types do not just arise from those criticizing inclusive research from the outside. Hugely experienced inclusive researcher Gordon Grant has reflected on this:

> What counts as knowledge? And what knowledge counts? . . . We are still stuck in this thing about hierarchies of evidence, peer reviewed, non peer reviewed, journal ranking, and all the rest of it . . . the inclusive research project is to me very much about relational practice, it's about pluralities of knowledge and people valuing and recognizing that and not putting one set of voices above another. (Oral contribution cited in Nind and Vinha, 2012, p. 34)

At least for this more nuanced position, the main criticism about the claim of inclusive research to more authentic knowledge is answered.

A second strand of criticism is that inclusive research assumes there is a standpoint shared by groups of researched people, and that inclusive research can add this previously missing standpoint. Todd (2012, p. 196) discusses the idea that the social production of knowledges (in the plural) 'is not the same as the linear addition of missing views that are regarded in more or less essentialist ways'. Citing Moore and Muller (1999), she is critical of a tendency among some researchers to reduce the kind of knowledge one holds to a single plane of experience, such as being a child. This relates to others' criticism of so-called standpoint epistemologies as '"naive" and dichotomising' (Mercer, 2002, cited by Warren and Boxall, 2009, p. 290). Such standpoint epistemologies are critiqued by Frankham (2009, p. 8) as conflating having an identity (such as woman) with holding a particular position (a woman's view). This, she says, is what Newman (2002) calls a 'bioessentialist assumption of a homogeneity of interests and identities' (Frankham, 2009, p. 12). The foolishness of this is apparent, she reminds us, when we consider that there is not always a straightforward distinction between service users and researchers. She gives the example of Peter Beresford – a professor and an 'out...mental health service user'; Staddon (2012), both an academic and with experience of alcohol misuse issues – represents another example of someone with insider/outsider identities. Edwards and Alexander (2011) offer their own research *on*, and *with*, lone mothers as an illustrative of how the concept of them as a coherent social group is misjudged. They also present another challenge to the oversimplistic nature of the insider/outsider dichotomy in their strategy to reach marginalized groups through university students from the same group. These peer researchers, they acknowledge, 'occupied a complex, "intermediate" position between the academy and the community' (p. 278).

Claims for superior, insider knowledge are related to claims that inclusive research, particularly that led by lay people, is (or should be) uncontaminated by academic and outsider standpoints. This is an extension of the essentialism discussed earlier. It is a widespread claim within the disabled people's movement and Kellett is a major proponent of it in children's research. She argues, for example, that 'children are party to the subculture of childhood which gives them a unique "insider" perspective that is critical to our understanding of children's worlds' (Kellett, 2005a, p. 4); she draws on Rousseau's eighteenth-century ideas about the 'purity of children's thought', their 'innate wisdom' and the 'essential core value of children's perspectives' (p. 9). She refers to '*genuine* child perspective' (p. 10, my emphasis), and the dangers of adults 'hi-jacking analysis and imposing adult interpretations' (p. 16). Thomson (2007, p. 208) counters this with a view of identities as fluid and multiple – 'constructed through a diverse web of overlapping subjectivities' with childhood being merely a 'socially produced category' with 'many voices' (p. 209).

Even if our identities were one-dimensional the essentialist leap to a particular understanding stemming from our position as woman, child, disabled, and so on is critiqued for assumptions about purity of voice and perspective. As Todd (2012, p. 96) argues, Bakhtin (1986) importantly points out: 'Our speech is filled with other's words, varying degrees of otherness or varying degrees of "our-own-ness".' This makes problematic the notion that by increasing people's participation in research, or using more creative participatory methods we are increasing our chances of accessing their 'authentic core being' (Bragg, 2010, p. 31, cited by Todd, 2012, p. 96). However much we are involved in research, this argument goes, our discourses (and knowledge) are produced by/within dominant discourses. Thomson and Gunter (2006, p. 852, again cited by Todd, 2012, p. 196) reflect on their research in schools, and state that 'having the right to speak and research did not mean that what was said by students was somehow any more "pure" or "authentic" than any other voices (including our own)'. Moreover, the influence of supporters on co-researchers may be impossible to eradicate and possibly 'just as evident in new paradigm research as in the traditional model' (Kiernan, 1999, p. 46).

Ultimately, Frankham (2009, pp. 16–17) sums up the criticism when she argues:

> [I]f personal experience is foregrounded it may be that rather than service users' knowledge being privileged, they become privileged as an (assumed) knower. That is, because they have had a particular experience they are assumed to understand that experience (not just be able to describe it). This may lead to an unfortunate 'taking at face value' everything that a service user describes.

In this way, 'there is a danger that in privileging the personal experience of individuals that new essentialisms will proliferate' (Frankham, 2009, p. 6). Individuals with valid knowledge about their personal experience come to represent whole groups of people who share a common characteristic with them. Their 'accounts, then, can act as a new form of ventriloquism – one person speaking for others – and to the homogenization of groups of people, as accepted accounts of what this experience means are repeated and reified' (p. 16). It is this concept of taking insider knowledge at face value, and being uncritical of the superiority and representativeness of it, that inclusive researchers need to grapple with for the sustainability and credibility of claims to an important research approach. As Grant (2013) asserts, different knowledges need to be tested as well as used.

Inclusive research is more ethical

Another core idea within inclusive research, and a claim made for it, is that it is in some inherent way more ethical than research in which participants provide data that researchers use (possibly exploiting the data and even the people themselves). Some inclusive researchers seek more nuanced positions. Holland et al. (2008), for example, recognize that participatory approaches are not alone in embedding research in an ethical framework and, furthermore, that research using such approaches have their own ethical complexities and sensitivities. Nonetheless, criticism of the basic claim that inclusive research is more ethical comes from inside and outside the field. Holland et al. (2008, p. 3) join with others in critiquing the notion that research which aims to be participatory is necessarily more enabling for participants, is ethically or morally superior to other types of research, or produces 'better' research', that it is 'unquestionably a "good thing"' (p. 20).

The criticism is both conceptually and practically based. Gallacher and Gallagher (2008, p. 501) make a conceptual case against participatory research and argue that it is 'important not to be distracted by the ethical allure of "empowerment", "agency" or "self-determination"'. Ethical considerations about power are discussed in the next section. Conolly (2008, pp. 204–5), in contrast, raises more pragmatic arguments that 'giving some socially excluded young women authority to conduct research on others raises a plethora of ethical issues', including that 'informed consent and confidentiality are more precarious when research is carried out by young people', who are sometimes willing to 'misuse knowledge and power bestowed upon them in the research situation'.

My view is that ethics are always contextually situated. Inclusive research contexts therefore have impact on the ethics of the situations experienced by individuals who are researchers/researched. Conolly (2008, p. 205) recognizes this when she makes assertions related to her own situation: '*In the context of my research*, I contend that engaging young people as co-researchers is at best unfeasible and at worst, somewhat unethical' (my emphasis). In inclusive contexts some ethical principles are foregrounded and positively addressed: it is unlikely that questions of who benefits from the research, who gets the credit for it, and who can access it, will not be at the forefront of the researchers' minds. However, other issues such as the roles and practices of those supporting but not leading research emerge as fresh and thorny ethical challenges.

Deciding to do research inclusively may be the start, rather than anywhere near the end, of the consideration of ethical issues that the researcher needs to do. Helpfully, the CCREC have set about addressing some of the ethical issues raised by collaborative or inclusive research, including what constitutes informed consent when the traditional researcher–researched boundaries are blurred or dissolved and what ethical dimensions emerge from equity-oriented research, which merges with civic action, 'given traditional university positions on political neutrality and disinterested scholarship' (CCREC, n.d.). Atkinson (2013) might add a question about what happens to lay people doing research when the research project ends. Her own experience has been that how and when to end her involvement with people with learning disabilities exploring their life stories presented a painful ethical dilemma. Edwards and Alexander (2011) also raise ethical questions about the relationships between community researchers and their communities after the research is over.

Inclusive research addresses the power imbalances between researcher and researched

Addressing the power relationship between the researcher and the researched is at the heart of inclusive research. One of the claims subjected to scrutiny is that inclusive research practices can and do disrupt or rupture the hierarchy of the powerful researcher and the powerless researched. Traditional power dynamics are uncomfortable for inclusive researchers who seek and sometimes assert that they have achieved a more democratic research relationship with those involved. These claims become emotive in situations when the researched have attempted to seize power or adopt radically different roles for themselves as producers of knowledge; those who critique the premise of this enter politically sensitive territory. Nonetheless, criticisms come from various standpoints.

One criticism of the claim for democratization is that moves towards this do not go far enough. Cornwall and Jewkes (1995, p. 669), for example, contend that much of what passes as participatory is still led, designed and managed by others. Participatory research approaches may be condemned by proponents of emancipatory research as merely tinkering at the edges rather than transforming the social relations of research production. Thus, Cahill (2007, p. 299) makes the case that 'participatory methods can reproduce rather than challenge unequal power relations' and, moreover, that use of the broad term participation 'often masks tokenism'. One of the dangers of children (and other lay people) adopting more active research roles is that they are – deliberately or inadvertently – co-opted to adopt professional viewpoints (Todd, 2012). As a discussant of Kellett's work observed, the more training given to lay researchers, the less like lay researchers they become as we teach them 'to look at the world through our lenses' (Nind et al., 2012). The cynical viewpoint is that this kind of inclusive research is more about 'active management than active citizenship' (Milewa et al., 1999, cited by Frankham, 2009, p. 13).

A more fundamental criticism concerning power sharing relates to the concept of power this reflects. Again Gallacher and Gallagher (2008) pull the metaphorical rug from under participatory research when they argue that the way in which power is largely positioned within it is fundamentally flawed. The problem arises when the power claim reflects a view of power as a 'commodity to be acquired, exchanged, shared and relinquished at will', 'transmitted by a set of predetermined techniques'. This is Kellett's (2011, p. 211) position: 'The power of child-child research is that it can transcend inequalities in power dynamics and propagate authentic insider perspectives.' Counter-arguments come from the Foucauldian position that power is exercised rather than possessed; like identities it is something we 'do' rather than 'have' (Thomson, 2007, after Butler, 1990). Edwards and Alexander (2011, p. 273) sum up the debate nicely:

> Power is posed as something that a group or individual has either more or less of, where those who have power can hand it over to (empower) those who have none. A more sophisticated consideration of power recognises that it is relational. Academic lead researchers cannot decide to transfer 'their' power to community researchers who then 'have' that power and can use it wherever and whenever. Rather, groups and individuals are subject to differing power potentials in different social relationships and contexts.

There is also seen to be a linked flaw in the logic concerning power, participation and competence in participatory research. Gallacher and Gallagher (2008) maintain that there is an internal inconsistency in the argument that (1) children are competent to be researchers and (2) that they need special participatory methods to engage them. Thomson (2007, p. 207) also notes this contradiction, previously highlighted by Punch (2002, p. 321): 'if children are competent social actors, why are special "child-friendly" methods needed to communicate with them?' Thomson (2007, p. 214) critiques the poor match 'between the bottom up political philosophy of participatory methodologies and the top down approach of pre-labelling participants prior to their entry into the research space'. This prelabelling involves a lot of assumptions about where power resides and why, as well as about who is competent.

A significant power differential between academic and lay researchers is that often the former is paid for their research and latter is not. This is a hugely sensitive power dynamic in some research and not easily resolved (Nind and Vinha, 2012); some funding councils want to see funds flow from university partners to their community partners in research projects, while others are very reluctant to fund adequately the lay people whose involvement they claim they value. This leads some academic researchers (and I include myself as 'guilty' of this) to accept an instrumental compromise position in which some participation without proper monetary reward is better than no participation at all. Some self-advocacy groups rely on the income from research to empower them to do other advocacy work; other inclusive researchers recognize some of the freedoms that come with not being tied by funders' agendas (Nind and Vinha, 2012). 'There can be a fine line between involving and empowering community members as peer researchers and exploiting their labour and expertise' (Edwards and Alexander, 2011, p. 273). There are different views on the outcomes of paying researchers as either part of the democratization of research or a means of instrumental control (see Edwards and Alexander, 2011) – 'buying' a level of compliance and accountability. The issues are made even more complex in the United Kingdom where, for many marginalized people, doing research brings with it practical tensions between being paid and claiming benefits.

Inclusive research is inclusive of people who have been silenced by traditional research

The rhetoric surrounding inclusive research includes a rhetoric that powerful researchers have silenced powerless others and that new research approaches can counter this. The truth in the former part of this is hard to dispute; what is more controversial is how far inclusive research can reach out to include and change things for such powerless groups. The territory has undoubtedly shifted – as we have seen, there are now research publications by children, people who are learning disabled, those with diagnoses of schizophrenia, and so on. As examples in Chapter 3 show, enormous social, material and communication barriers to becoming involved in research have been overcome through PAR designs and visual methods, for example. Thus groups of people previously marginalized in research are more visible and valued, their voices and particular grounded forms of knowledge are included, and so the claims for research contributing to a more inclusive society can be understood.

Some of the critique of inclusivity comes from those who question the extent to which the inclusion of minority voices can and has been achieved. One critique relates to who gets to do inclusive research. Holland et al. (2008, p. 6) rehearse this critique and the viewpoint that only some individuals from various marginalized groups want to get involved. In this way it is those who want to be a good citizen or who are 'emotionally literate' who become heard within inclusive research. The boundary of inclusion may broaden, but only so far. There are limits to the extent to which research will ever stop reflecting a certain (white, middle-class) form of communication and so those willing and able to adopt this are privileged in inclusive research, as in any research. Cornwall and Jewkes (1995) note that understandably there are barriers in terms of the time and motivation that many ordinary people have available for research which inevitably limits their inclusion in it. This means that some people are easier to recruit as participants or co-researchers than others. Among people with learning disabilities, it is those who have already been empowered through self-advocacy work who are well positioned to become researchers (McLarty and Gibson, 2000; Johnson, 2009). Conolly (2008) argues that those who are most socially excluded become those who remain excluded from research.

There is a viable counter-argument here. This centres on the resources available for research. Inclusive researchers have shown the necessity of funds and time to facilitate meaningful inclusion (Nind and Vinha, 2012). Conolly (2008) notes that the unreliability of young people in difficult circumstances is particularly problematic if research budgets and timelines are tight; while we cannot change the reality of the young people's lives being fragmented and transitory, there are some things that researchers can do to deal with the challenges this presents. It could be said that we are only beginning to understand what can be achieved in terms of drawing people into research in new ways. With more time and more resources more is likely to be achievable. This raises the debate about the cost-benefit analysis of inclusive research – how much are we willing to invest for what outcomes? There are also questions about how broadly we are willing to expand our concept of research. There have been efforts to include people with profound impairments and limited non-verbal communication, but the level and kind of involvement and emancipation possible (e.g. through interpreting video-recorded potentially communicative behaviour (McLarty and Gibson, 2000)) may stretch the limits of the concept beyond breaking point.

There are limits to what inclusive research can achieve. This is in part because some important research agendas may be neglected as not being on the horizons of children (Conolly, 2008; Nind et al., 2012) or other lay researchers, and because not all topics are amenable to emancipatory approaches (Kiernan, 1999). It is also because not everyone wants to be involved in research as Johnson (2009) found in her attempts to include learning disabled people in research in Ireland. This reluctance can also arise for potential participants who are involved in illegal, taboo or stigmatized practices. This means inclusive research is left in a position where a heterogeneity of voices is not well represented by the few and, as Kellett (2010, pp. 31–2) argues, where we have to guard against a vocal and articulate few monopolizing the research agenda while 'hard-to-reach groups languish on the margins'. This is a pertinent reality for inclusive research in the learning/disability field where, despite massive advances in what has been achieved in drawing people into valued research roles, those with profound or multiple impairments and the informal carers who are also oppressed by their situations have made minimal inroads on the new paradigm (Kiernan, 1999). This is true also of those people not already empowered in advocacy/community groups. The extent to which the limits to the scope of inclusive research can be made into a case against it is largely a matter for individual opinion, but it is mostly problematic if a new elite group replaces an old elite group (Danieli and Woodhams, 2005) as this would bring the whole movement into question.

Inclusive (particularly emancipatory) research is empowering

The next area for critical debate concerns the claim that people used to being objects of investigation become empowered, bringing about a transformation in their lives (Fielding, 2004). To recap, this is about the empowerment potential of setting one's own research agenda, leading one's own research and developing skills, networks, political agency, confidence and self-esteem (Kellett, 2005a) as one understands one's situation through research (Johnson, 2009). There is debate among those involved in inclusive research about who can do the empowering of the participants. If would-be participants do not become the researchers, they remain participants who cannot be empowered by the researcher or necessarily empower themselves (Thomson, 2007). This relates to the criticism that power is not a commodity to be passed or shared around and to an awareness of the 'possible disempowering potentials of research' (Todd, 2012, p. 191).

Some of the arguments about the claims of empowerment stem from a failure among those claiming it to actually theorize or even define it: ' "Mere invocation is, seemingly, thought to suffice" ' (Frankham, 2009, p. 21, citing McLaren and Giarelli, 1995, p. 301). Danieli and Woodhams (2005) present a strong critique focused on the dominance of emancipatory research in disability studies. They assert that 'the advocacy of emancipatory research is itself an exercise of power which can result in the silencing of some voices' (p. 282). They argue for separation of emancipation and participation as concepts. This is endorsed by Todd (2012, p. 197), who argues that 'there is no simple equating of the greater involvement of children in research with progress and social justice'. Danieli and Woodhams (2005, p. 290) draw on developments in feminist research in which feminists have reached what they regard as a more nuanced position: 'For many feminists, the solution to the dilemmas posed by emancipatory research has been in the de-coupling of participation and emancipation. In other words, it is recognised that knowledge that can be used to emancipate women's lives does not always require a particular methodological approach to achieve political objectives.' This, they argue, avoids the problem of limiting the people who get to do research and those who get heard to those who conform to a particular view of who is the expert in research. Ultimately, their problem is more with the strong push for emancipatory research rather than the claim that such research is empowering, but the two do become conjoined.

In weighing up arguments about whether claims made for inclusive research being empowering are exaggerated, it is worth remembering that many inclusive researchers aspire to this rather than claim it as reality. Moreover, it is relative to what has gone before, not some absolute universal standard. Even Oliver (1997) has recognized that the power of research to be emancipatory has to be judged after the event. It may well be that judgements about whether research empowers individuals or emancipates groups is best left to those individuals and groups. This is the argument that empowerment can best be judged from the inside, though an understanding of Freire's (1970) emphases on praxis and dialogue (see Chapter 3) adds layers of complexity here.

Inclusive research is a panacea

Collectively, those who commission, conduct and use inclusive research ask a lot of it (Nind and Vinha, 2012, 2013). It may be that in wanting research to be so transformative, of people, societal problems and ways of knowing, that we are actually asking too much of it. Smith (2012, p. xiii), for example, has argued that a research agenda defined by indigenous people might build capacity and work towards 'healing, reconciliation and development'. Edwards and Alexander (2011, p. 273) argue that expecting community-led or involved research to bring about positive social change is to place 'an unrealistic, even cruelly misleading, burden' on lay researchers. As an expression of our distaste with how research has sometimes been conducted it may be that we expect inclusive research to be a panacea for so many research ills – *and* perform some therapeutic role. There are, inevitably, conceptual and practical problems with this.

Conceptually, questions are raised about just how different inclusive research is from qualitative research, which by its nature already gives voice to participants (Gallacher and Gallagher, 2008). Equally, the idea of shifting notions of who is expert is problematized, with Gallacher and Gallagher (2008, p. 511) proposing instead that we should 'abandon the very notion of "expertise", instead positioning all researchers as "emergent-becomings – always-unfinished subjects-in-the-making – humans cannot claim to be experts: to be fully knowing, competent and rational"'. Some inclusive researchers, inside and outside the academy, do recognize their immaturity as researchers and their fallibility. Nonetheless this line of argument is an important one in that 'participatory methods are in danger of being seen as a "fool-proof" technology that – when applied carefully and conscientiously – will enable research involving children [or others] to achieve ethical and epistemological validity' (p. 513). It is salutary to reflect on the conclusion of Gallacher and Gallagher (2008, p. 513) that 'participatory methods are no less problematic, or ethically ambiguous, than any other research method . . . [not] inherently any better, or worse, that any other research method.'

Adopting an inclusive approach or participatory methods, it is argued, must not be a response to them being available as options, popular at a particular time or in a particular field or popular with a particular group of 'neglected others' (Todd, 2012, p. 192). Methods and approaches must fit the question and not just be used because they are participatory, creative or innovative (Nind et al., 2012). It is not helpful for the hurt at historical/traditional research practices to silence critical dialogue about new research practices, such as when and how they are appropriate, enriching or problematic. It is therefore important that inclusive research approaches are discussed and debated, rather than becoming the unquestionable new orthodoxy (Walmsley and Johnson, 2003). Dialogue is needed which engages multiple voices to get to new understandings we could not reach alone (Nind and Vinha, 2013). This is a premise in inclusive research and can be usefully applied to it – to the conceptual and the practical. In some fields, such as child-led research, the conceptual has been underdeveloped and debated in comparison with the practical (Nind et al., 2012) while in others, such as learning disability research, practical challenges have been glossed over (Walmsley and Johnson, 2003).

Clement (2003, cited by Walmsley and CEPF, in press) refers to the amount of 'claims making' in writing about self-advocacy, that is, 'saying what is important while not explaining the conditions which support its success; nor its challenges and difficulties'. This could also be said of inclusive research. It has meant that the idea of inclusive research as a panacea has gained strength while simultaneously some areas of research and debate have been neglected as too difficult to make inclusive. Fear of getting it wrong is rife in fields where there is a strong culture of inclusive research and the idea, discussed earlier, of us all being immature researchers in development may be used to counter this. The publication of reflexive accounts helps to counter this fear; as researchers are honest about the compromises they make and the pragmatic decision making that is needed, and so on, they challenge the aura that perfect inclusion is necessary or possible.

Also related to the panacea idea, claims about the relative impact that inclusive research can make are challenged: 'a number of critics have pointed out the naivety of the notion that traditional research is without value because it does not result in immediate change in the material and social conditions of people with disability' (Kiernan, 1999, p. 45). Shakespeare (1996) is sceptical that participatory or emancipatory research will bring about policy change. Kiernan (1999) notes how impact is complex and often happens slowly through cultural change. Fisher and Robinson (2010, p. 209) endorse this, arguing that actively engaging lay/ disabled people in social policy research 'takes longer' 'and requires a delicate balance between the stakeholders'. They reflect on their practical experience with this and the need for a longitudinal, formative approach to shaping policy implementation, governed not by service users but by participatory principles with multiple formal and informal approaches making it possible. Service users' data, which was about lived experience, for them was 'a touchstone from which other data could be measured' (p. 216), but working to make impact still involved managing conflicting interests and diffusing potential hostilities between participants. Inclusive research, it seems, may not solve the impact issue but it can add new dimensions to it.

Sometimes the most emancipatory/user-led research is presented as the pinnacle (Kellett, 2005a). Involvement in the dialogic processes of *Doing Research Inclusively, Doing Research Well?* (Nind and Vinha, 2012) led Hilra Vinha and me to question this stance and to see greater value in a more collaborative model. In such interdependent research no-one becomes a pawn in a political battle (Kiernan, 1999) and no voices are suppressed. Research problems are worked through in principled and practical ways, putting the pressures surrounding claims making in their place – secondary to the importance of the research. Doing research inclusively does not solve the issue of who can speak for whom as much as raise new questions about this. Clark (2001, p. 334) reflects on this in rela- tion to the Mosaic approach: 'We did not want to set up a framework for listening which ignored or undervalued the insights of those who spend their lives with young children, but to find new ways for adults to reflect on these perspectives with the children themselves.' Those involved in inclusive research are required to learn how to play their part, sometimes reversing or minimizing their conventional roles (Yardley, 2011) or to see themselves as a resource or consultant (Johnson, 2009). This may require training or practice (Coad and Evans, 2008). In the case of, for example, non-disabled supporters their essential roles may be 'hidden and obscure', thereby evading 'honest reflection' (Walmsley, 2004, p. 65). However, as supporting inclusive research is, as Walmsley (p. 66) argues, such a 'skilled activity' the sustainability and development of inclusive research requires greater transparency about the skills involved and how they are fostered.

Acting with self-restraint may be unappealing to conventional researchers and support workers, but acting in sensitively skilled and subtle ways using 'finely honed skills' (p. 69) could be more attractive and more empowering.

Summary

To summarize, it can be difficult to criticize inclusive research without seeming to criticize democratic principles or the people from minority groups who stand to benefit. Nonetheless, debates do rage about what counts as inclusive research, when it is good enough, whether it is worth pursuing, inherent conceptual confusions and practical realities. Like all kinds of research it needs to be considered with a critical and reflexive openness to explore the role it might play in particular socio-cultural contexts and in addressing particular research problems.

5 Summary and where next? The pursuit of quality in inclusive research

I began this book by showing that describing 'what is inclusive research' is not straightforward. Inclusive research encompasses a range of research practices conducted for a range of reasons, but with some fundamental principles and frustrations in common with other kinds of research. In Chapter 2, I have shown the diverse influences on the development of inclusive research as an overarching concept, the development of the specific concepts of emancipatory, participatory, participatory action and the development of partnership/user-led/child-led research. The various drivers at work were illustrated by the examples in Chapter 3 where I have tried to bring the diversity of inclusive research to life. I have then taken us through the various debates within the field, the criticisms waged at the concepts and practices and the defences offered. In this final chapter, I focus on where inclusive research has got to and how the future might unfold. This is no less controversial than the material that has gone before and no less dependent on one's standpoint.

The state of the art of inclusive research

I do not wish to repeat the content of earlier chapters, but it is helpful at this juncture to list some of the achievements in the field of inclusive research alongside some of the challenges. This reflects my own analysis of where we are. This, in turn, is based on my own position as researcher with particular interests in social and educational inclusion, in methodology, and in the social and communication worlds of people with learning disabilities (stemming from earlier professional interest as a teacher). I am someone who does research *on*, *with* and *for* people with learning disabilities (and also other learners, educationalists and researchers). I have a strong interest in doing research inclusively, but I am not exclusively allied to it. (I deliberately use this phrase *doing research inclusively* with the active verb, preferring it to the apparently more fixed *inclusive research*, as it implies greater flexibility.) I am not immune to the ethical or moral allure of inclusive research, but I think we need to come to know it critically, not superficially. The analysis in this chapter is also based on my extensive involvement with this field of research and on the recent completion of *Doing Research Inclusively, Doing Research Well?* (Nind and Vinha, 2012) in which I had the privilege of engaging in extended dialogue with experienced people conducting inclusive research in all kinds of ways. I am therefore fascinated by the intricacies and nuances of interpreting inclusive principles in action and, particularly as a result of the recent study, persuaded that inclusive research needs to remain vibrant, fluid and the subject of further dialogue (Nind and Vinha, 2013).

I set out some of the achievements and challenges in Table 5.1.

Dialogue in inclusive research

It is clear when we stand back and look at inclusive research that its full potential is yet to be realized. There are plenty more twists and turns to be travelled in its development. There is much to be gained from making constructive use of the frictions in the field to understand it better. There is plenty to be learned too from more engagement across the different conceptualizations of particular approaches under the umbrella of inclusive research, as researchers working with each of these are relatively unaware of each other's work. There are also potential benefits to be gained from dialogue across substantive areas so that, for example, researchers in community LGBT groups are talking to advocates of child-led research and to people with and without labels of learning disability who collaborate in research. Particularly important is 'frank and open debate ... untrammelled by unhelpful dogmatizing' (Walmsley and Johnson, 2003, p. 16). We went some way towards constructive dialogue with inclusive researchers in the learning disability field in the *Doing Research Inclusively, Doing Research Well?* focus groups. Here we used dialogue as Freire (1970) suggests 'as a means of understanding and transforming – reflecting and acting' (Nind and Vinha, 2013, p. 6). Nonetheless, while some participant-researchers embraced the opportunities for learning from and with each other, accepting that there is no right way to do inclusive research, others were more comfortable with their own sense of expertise and preferred to assert their views about what inclusive research *should* be like. This limited the extent

Table 5.1 State of the art of inclusive research

Achievements	Challenges
The need for inclusive research has become recognized in government policies that embrace service user involvement.	Such government policies lack a clear vision of what is meant by inclusive research.
The rhetoric about ordinary people in their diversity needing to enjoy rights, choices, inclusion, citizenship and involvement in services/decisions affecting them is well established.	The implications of this in research terms are underexplored.
The high profile of the importance of collaborations between academic researchers and those they research is influencing the choices made by pure and applied qualitative researchers.	The implications of this for our understanding of high-quality social science research are underexplored.
There is a growing interest in the impact of involving lay people in research related to them. Evidence of positive and negative impacts on the public, the lay people involved, the researchers and the research is beginning to be gathered and reviewed.	This is partly concerned with justifying the additional time and cost. The difficulties in evaluating impact and making comparisons are considerable.
The additional time and costs involved in doing research inclusively are increasingly recognized.	The economic and non-economic costs and benefits related to participation in research of service users/lay researchers are little understood.
Supporters of inclusive research have created a positive association between involvement in research and social inclusion more generally.	This is largely still at the level of claims making with supporting evidence beginning to emerge. Policy is ahead of good scientific knowledge in this respect.
Previously excluded or marginalized people are becoming recognized as social actors/change agents and gaining benefits from their new socially valued roles.	The long-term benefits are unknown and there are indications that new roles may be short-lived.
Inclusive research is being commissioned and funded by respected sources, indicating the acceptance by that this is valid research.	Only a minority of funding bodies and research programmes have ventured down this path; they are learning as they go along.

Continued

Table 5.1 Continued

Achievements	Challenges
Users of services and people whose voices have traditionally not been heard, who have felt some anger or distrust of their treatment by services and research, have begun to take a role in the following: shaping research priorities; commissioning research; evaluating research tenders; advising on research; conducting research; publishing research; teaching research methods; peer-reviewing research.	These roles are largely limited to individuals who have already sought to have a voice through organized community action. Those individuals are grappling with huge social and material challenges.
There have been huge advances in our practical knowledge about how to make the research process, and the products of research, more accessible to lay people.	Participatory methods are less well developed and reported for data analysis compared with data collection. There may be most potential for participatory data analysis when the boundaries between data collection and data analysis are blurred and the process is organic.
Participation varies; there co-exists claims to genuine participation throughout the whole research process and accusations of tokenism.	The extent of participation can become a preoccupation and a distraction from how participation is achieved and to what effect.
Rhetoric about researching in partnership is rife.	Researchers, co-researchers, supporters and allies are actively negotiating what partnership actually means in their research contexts.
There is much variation in the terms used to describe people doing inclusive research including: co-researchers, lay researchers, learner researchers, participant-researchers, experts by experience.	The variation in terms reflects fluidity in concepts, diversity of backgrounds, political sensitivities, and a general lack of certainty in what is still a new field.
Different kinds of knowledge and ways of knowing are being valued, including the grounded knowledge that has historically been missed or dismissed.	The status of knowledge grounded in everyday experience is somewhat troubled, ranging from being reified as expert knowledge to being subjected to expert analysis by others.
There are many rich reports of inclusive research and some reflections on the inclusive research process.	Often reports lack detail on how participation was optimized and critical self-reflection and shared reflection are needed.

Table 5.1 Continued

Achievements	Challenges
There is emerging guidance on managing ethics in inclusive research.	Developments like this in CBPR are not quickly or automatically known or applied by inclusive researchers working under a different label, e.g. child-led research or participatory health research.
Training on how to do inclusive research is emerging and some of this includes the pursuit of quality.	Spaces for reflexive thinking about inclusive research can be constrained by the political sensitivities. Fear and accusations about getting it wrong can limit engagement with theoretical and pragmatic criticisms.
There are celebratory narratives surrounding inclusive research and the added value it can bring.	We are only just beginning to understand how to assess quality in inclusive research and how to judge its worth in light of the multiple things asked of it.

to which, in some focus groups, people's assumptions were troubled. It may be that in other fields the ground is less sensitive and there is less wariness about causing conflict or offence. Even so, this communal process of reflection highlighted the many different ways in which people work together as inclusive researchers, making sensitive judgements and taking considered actions, committed to the principle that research should be done *by*, *with* or *for* people, but not simply *on* them. The intellectual and physical space to discuss this was welcomed and notions about what made our research inclusive and good gradually became more refined.

Quality in inclusive research

When I discussed the debates and controversies surrounding inclusive research in Chapter 4, I did not interrogate the question of what constitutes quality in inclusive research. This is because this is rarely discussed in any depth in the literature about any of the kinds of inclusive research approach. The starting point is often that it is better, has greater potential or meets a particular need (Minkler, 2005). Staley (2009), though, when interrogating the question of impact, recognizes the complexities of evaluating the impact made when research that breaks traditions and norms to increase user involvement. This field has a hidden subtext in which in various studies the level of participation is said to be weak or superficial and these are assumed to be poor examples of inclusive research, but this is not quite the same as judging the research to be of poor quality; the converse is equally true. Yet there is also a sense in which the quality of the participation and the quality of the research sit in a kind of tension. Criteria for what makes research good quality from a traditional social science perspective are unlikely to be the first things that come to mind when service users/lay researchers talk about what makes research good from their perspective.

The CCREC (n.d.) recognize the knowledge and knowing dimension of collaborative/inclusive research as an ethical as well as quality issue. They include in their questions for interrogation in developing a code of ethics for collaborative research, 'How should the epistemic standing of research partners and participants be respected while also meeting established research norms that warrant findings?' Similarly, Edwards and Alexander (2011, p. 272) question assumptions about community involvement leading to better data, arguing instead that 'there may be "trade-offs" between research quality and empowerment' when community (lay) researchers are involved. They break the tradition of celebrating the special qualities of peer researchers as interviewers with examples of poor practice, lacking in rigour. This 'trade-off' idea is applied more generally to the matter of balancing what insider and outsider researchers bring to the process; Edwards and Alexander (2011) are explicit that insider, peer researchers can damage as well as enhance quality through their (over)familiarity with the research context or problem. Potential for such negative impact is endorsed in Staley's (2009) review, where other negative as well as positive impacts are discussed, though Staley reminds us that many of the former are avoidable with more support and training.

Lather (1986) reminds us of the need to disrupt normative criteria for quality in research and that validity equates with power. She reflects on how qualitative concepts of quality have evolved to be more fluid, blending rigour and ethics and she nominates face validity and catalytic validity as especially suited to new paradigm research and the concern with transformation through understanding for those involved. The quality question was one of the conundrums that we focused on in *Doing Research Inclusively, Doing Research Well?* (Nind and Vinha, 2012). Specifically, one of our research questions was about what makes a piece of research good for people judging it for its research and for its inclusive qualities – when do good social science and good inclusive research come together? The dialogue about this was productive and ultimately, after time immersed in the focus group transcripts, we could see that collectively we could understand that quality is recognizable in research *and* inclusivity terms when:

1. the research answers questions we could not otherwise answer, but that are important,
2. the research reaches participants, communities and knowledge, in ways that we could not otherwise access,
3. the research involves using and reflecting on the insider, cultural knowledge of people with learning disabilities,
4. the research is authentic (recognized by the people involved),
5. the research makes an impact on the lives of people with learning disabilities. (Nind and Vinha, 2012, pp. 43–4)

In this set of circumstances the research would be valued by funding councils and self-advocates alike. Matters of relevance, design and methods that are the best fit for purpose, reflexively considering different ways of knowing and making an impact come together to provide a framework through which we might judge quality in inclusive research. This does not equate with prescribing how it should be conducted. This was not the purpose of the study and it is not the purpose of this book. There are many useful texts that take the reader through *how to do* inclusive research and these are outlined in the section on further reading and resources. Understanding what inclusive research is and what quality means in inclusive research are more fundamental challenges. Cook (2012) cites the argument of Wright et al. (2010) that this is important if we are to avoid the situation in which each participatory research proposal needs to be argued and judged on its own terms. She sees value in establishing a uniting paradigm so that such 'repeated individual justification' (para 44) becomes unnecessary and argues:

> The responsibility for ensuring that participatory research is judged according to its own merits, and that it finds appropriate and powerful spaces to make a difference to current practice, lies in two courts, those of participatory researchers and those who review participatory research. If the first step is to be more explicit about the nature, purpose and potential of the paradigm within which

we work, the ball is currently in our side of the court. Participatory research faces the challenge of establishing its credentials. (para 60)

Here I merely represent in Table 5.2 the guidance generated in *Doing Research Inclusively, Doing Research Well?* which to some extent operationalizes quality indicators without being prescriptive. As we clarify in the research report (Nind and Vinha, 2012) there is no formula for turning the answers to these questions into some kind of quality score – this is a trigger for reflection and discussion only – because, when it comes to understanding inclusive research, we are still learning. This viewpoint is endorsed by ICPHR in that they anticipate that any framework they produce for quality in participatory health research 'would not be rigid, but rather serve as an aid to informed judgement' (Springett et al., 2011, p. 1). It should be noted that, while these questions (Table 5.2) are worded in relation to research with people with learning disabilities as in their original form, they could apply to any group.

Table 5.2 Questions to ask yourself when judging the quality of inclusive research with people with learning disabilities

1	Is the topic relevant to the lives of people with learning disabilities and interesting to them? Could it become relevant?
2	Does the research involve people with learning disabilities in a meaningful and active way?
3	Are the participants in the research treated with respect?
4	Is the research communicated in a way people with learning disabilities can understand and respond to?
5	Is there honesty and transparency about everyone's role and contribution?
6	Were the ways of working carefully thought through and adapted in response to needs?
7	Does the research create worthwhile knowledge?
8	Are there likely long-term wider benefits for the people involved, e.g. new networks, skills, funds, roles, social inclusion?
9	Are the research questions the kind that inclusive research can best answer?
10	Does the research reach participants, communities and knowledge that other research could not reach?
11	Does the research use, and reflect on, the insider cultural knowledge of people with learning disabilities?
12	Is the research genuine and meaningful?
13	Will the research make impact that people with learning disabilities value?

Other groups of researchers are beginning to tackle the matter of quality in inclusive research. ICPHR (2013, p. 20), looking at this in relation to participatory health research, follow Patti Lather in identifying the different concepts of validity (in the sense of achieving what one sets out to achieve) that might be usefully applied in an evaluative context:

- *Participatory Validity*. The extent to which all stakeholders are able to take an active part in the research process to the full extent possible.
- *Intersubjective Validity*. The extent to which the research is viewed as being credible and meaningful by the stakeholders from a variety of perspectives.
- *Contextual Validity*. The extent to which the research relates to the local situation.
- *Catalytic Validity*. The extent to which the research is useful in terms of presenting new possibilities for social action.
- *Ethical Validity*. The extent to which the research outcomes and the changes exerted on people by the research are sound and just.
- *Empathic Validity*. The extent to which the research has increased empathy among the participants.

Rahman (1991) stresses the need for people to select or create their own verification system to have control of the legitimacy of their knowledge. Nonetheless, the concepts listed here are all familiar and have been addressed in the book, albeit not always with these labels.

Cook (2012, para 11) sums up some of the core concepts when she discusses the qualities of/quality in inclusive research as involving co-labouring, citing Sumara and Luce-Kapler's (1993, p. 393) description of this involving 'toil, distress, trouble'. For her, good participatory research builds communities of practice (Wenger, 1998), with working interactions that 'harness a dynamic interchange of knowledge and understanding' (para 11). She concludes, 'What is important in participatory research is not existing "hierarchies of credibility" (Winter, 1998, p. 57) but mutual learning and emergent knowledge' (para 11). All these concepts are most helpful in steering a reviewer to questions of whether the research meets the qualities desired of participatory or inclusive research, perhaps more so than in judging whether the research is good quality per se.

Conclusion

The key messages I choose to leave the reader to consider are as follows:

- Inclusive research means different things to different people. It is a useful term to embrace a range of research approaches that share some common aspirations.
- There is no single right way to do inclusive research. There is conceptual confusion and pluralism as well as a multitude of practices.
- There is a need for honesty, transparency, realism and detail when we report how we go about doing research inclusively; different contributions to research should be 'named and described and recognized for what they are, not for what we wish they could be' (Walmsley, 2004, p. 69).
- It is possible to move towards understanding how good social science and good inclusive research can co-exist. Achieving this is challenging but necessary, and may take time.
- 'Fear of doing it [inclusive research] badly should not prevent us from attempting it' (Sin and Fong, 2010, p. 21).

This book has been about what inclusive research is. I recognize and value inclusive research as a helpful term. As I alluded to briefly earlier in this chapter, my own preference, however, is to refer instead to doing research inclusively (Nind and Vinha, 2012, 2013). This moves us away somewhat from the categorical process of labelling an approach or family of approaches in research. Instead, it places the emphasis on the entity being dynamic and in evolution – renegotiated to fit each unique research situation. My own relationship with inclusive research is shifting and the less it is seen as static or prescribed the more comfortable with it I am.

Further reading and resources

For guidance on how to do inclusive research, readers might find the following sources helpful.

Research with children and young people

International Journal of Social Research Methodology, 15(2), 2012, special issue on Creative Methods with Young People.
Child Indicators Research, 4(2), 2011, special issue on Children as Experts in Their Lives: Child Inclusive Research.

Various books contain step-by-step guidance, tips, case studies or useful resource material for researchers planning to conduct research *with* children and young people – examples include:

- Kellett, M. (2005), *How to Develop Children as Researchers*, London: Sage.
- Kellett, M. (2010), *Rethinking Children and Research: Attitudes in Contemporary Society*, London: Continuum.
- McCabe, A. and Horsley, K. (2008), *The Evaluator's Cookbook*, London: Routledge.
- Tisdall, E. K. M., Davis, J. M. and Gallagher, M. (2009), *Researching with Children and Young People: Research Design, Methods and Analysis*, London: Sage.

Useful online resources can be found at:
www.open.ac.uk/researchprojects/childrens-research-centre

Following their *Beyond Tokenism* conference in 2011 the National Children's Bureau published *Guidelines for Research with Children and Young People* (by C. Shaw, L.-M. Brady and C. Davey) available at: www.ncb.org.uk/media/434791/guidelines_for_research_with_cyp.pdf

Research with learning/disabled people

British Journal of Learning Disabilities, 40(2), 2012, special issue on the Research and Work of Learning Disabled People with Their Allies and Supporters.

Journal of Applied Research in Intellectual Disabilities, forthcoming, special issue on New Directions in Inclusive Research.

Social Work Education, 31(2), 2012, special issue on Disability Studies and Social Work Education.

Useful resources available online include:

Let Me In – I'm a Researcher! by the Learning Difficulties Research Team and published by the Department of Health. This is a report on the ways in which research commissioned following the Valuing People White Paper succeeded, or otherwise, in being inclusive www.dh.gov.uk/en/Publicationsandstatistics/Publications/PublicationsPolicyAndGuidance/DH_4132916

Doing Research Inclusively, Doing Research Well? by M. Nind and H. Vinha reports on research about quality in inclusive research with people with learning disabilities following focus groups with inclusive researchers. The report includes case study materials and these and video resources are available at:
www.doingresearchinclusively.org

The inclusive research network is in development, see:
www.inclusiveresearch.net/doing-inclusive-research

Inclusive research in other domains

International Journal of Social Research Methodology, 16(6), 2011, special issue on Perspectives on Decolonizing Methodologies.

International Journal of Social Research Methodology, 12(2), 2009, special issue on New Methods in Social Justice Research for the 21st Century.

Other useful guidance material available online includes:

Faulkner, A. (2005), *Guidance for Good Practice: Service User Involvement in UK Mental Health Research Network*, UK Mental Health Research Network.
www.mhrn.info/data/files/FOR_RESEARCHERS/Service_user_involvement_Good_Practice_2006.pdf

Resources developed by INVOLVE regarding public involvement in health and social care research:
www.invo.org.uk/resource-centre/resource-for-researchers

References

Acker, J., Barry, K. and Esseveld, J. (1991), 'Objectivity and Truth, Problems of Doing Feminist Research', in M. M. Fonow and J. A. Cook (eds), *Beyond Methodology: Feminist Scholarship as Lived Research*, Bloomington and Indianapolis: Indiana University Press.

Ackermann, L., Feeny, T., Hart, J. and Newman, J. (2003), *Understanding and Evaluating Children's Participation*, London: Plan UK/Plan International.

Alcoff, L. (1992), 'The Problem of Speaking for Others', *Cultural Critique*, 20: 5–32.

Aspis, S. (2000), 'Researching Our Own History: Who Is in Charge?' in L. Brigham, D. Atkinson, M. Jackson, S. Rolph and J. Walmsley (eds), *Crossing Boundaries: Change and Continuity in the History of Learning Disabilities*, Kidderminster: BILD.

Atkinson, D. (2013), 'Practical and Emotional Issues in Co-Researching', *Towards Equal and Active Citizenship: Pushing the Boundaries of Participatory Research with People with Learning Disabilities*, ESRC Seminar series, University of Plymouth, January.

Ayrton, R. (2012), 'The Bead Method: A Biographical Approach to Researching Mothers and Trust in Post-War South Sudan', *MethodsNews*, Winter: 6 <http://eprints.ncrm.ac.uk/2923/1/MethodsNewsWinter2012.pdf> [accessed 1 February 2013].

Bakhtin, M. M. (1986), *The Dialectical Imagination: Four Essays* (M. Holquist, ed.), Austin, TX: University of Texas Press.

Barnes, C. (2003), 'What a Difference a Decade Makes: Reflections on Doing "Emancipatory" Disability Research', *Disability and Society*, 18(1): 3–17.

Bennett, F. (2004), *Participatory Approaches to Research on Poverty*, York: Joseph Rowntree Foundation.

Beresford, P. (2002), 'User Involvement in Research and Evaluation: Liberation or Regulation?' *Social Policy and Society*, 1(2): 95–105.

Beresford, P. and Carr, S. (2012), 'Conclusion: The Personal Is Still Political', in P. Beresford and S. Carr (eds), *Social Care, Service Users and User Involvement*, London: Jessica Kingsley.

Beresford, P. and Wallcraft, J. (1997), 'Psychiatric System Survivors and Emancipatory Research: Issues, Overlaps and Differences', in C. Barnes and G. Mercer (eds), *Doing Disability Research*, Leeds: Disability Press.

Bjornsdottir, K. and Svensdottir, A. S. (2008), 'Gambling for Capital: Learning Disability, Inclusive Research and Collaborative Life Histories', *British Journal of Learning Disabilities*, 36: 263–70.

Booth, T. and Booth, W. (1996), 'Sounds of Silence: Narrative Research with Inarticulate Subjects', *Disability and Society*, 11: 55–69.

Bourdieu, P. (1984), *Distinction: A Social Critique of the Judgement of Taste*, Cambridge: Cambridge University Press.

Bourke, L. (2009), 'Reflections on Doing Participatory Research in Health: Participation, Method and Power', *International Journal of Social Research Methodology*, 12(5): 457–74.

Bowles, G. and Duelli Klein, R. (eds) (1983), *Theories of Women's Studies*, London: Routledge and Kegan Paul.

Boxall, K., Warren, L. and Chau, R. (2007), 'User Involvement', in S. M. Hodgson and Z. Irving (eds), *Policy Reconsidered. Meanings, Politics and Practices*, Bristol: Policy Press.

Bragg, S. (2010), *Consulting Young People: A Literature Review*, 2nd edn, Newcastle upon Tyne: Creativity, Culture and Education.

British Journal of Learning Disabilities (2012), Special issue on the 'Research and Work of Learning Disabled People with Their Allies and Supporters', 40(2): 83–164.

Browne, K., Bakshi, L. and Lim, J. (2012), '"There's No Point in Doing Research if No One Wants to Listen" Identifying LGBT Needs and Effecting "Positive Social Change" for LGBT People in Brighton and Hove', in P. Beresford and S. Carr (eds), *Social Care, Service Users and User Involvement*, London: Jessica Kingsley.

Burke, P. J. and Kirton, A. (2006), 'The Insider Perspective: Teachers-as-Researchers', *Reflecting Education*, 2(1): 1–4.

Butler, J. (1990), *Gender Trouble: Feminism and the Subversion of Identity*, London: Routledge.

Byers, R., Davies, J., Fergusson, A. and Marvin, C. (2008), *What About Us? Promoting Emotional Well-Being for Young People with Learning Disabilities in Inclusive Schools and Colleges: Project Report*, Cambridge/

London: University of Cambridge Faculty of Education/Foundation for People with Learning Disabilities.

Byrne, A., Canavan, J. and Millar, M. (2009), 'Participatory Research and the Voice-Centred Relational Method of Data Analysis: Is It Worth It?' *International Journal of Social Research Methodology*, 12(1): 67–77.

Cahill, C. (2007), 'Doing Research with Young People: Participatory Research and the Rituals of Collective Work', *Children's Geographies*, 5(3): 297–312.

Cancian, F. (1989), 'Participatory Research and Working Women: Democratizing the Production of Knowledge', paper presented at the Annual Meeting of the American Sociological Association, September, San Francisco.

Carr, W. and Kemmis, S. (2009), 'Educational Action Research: A Critical Approach', in S. Noffke and B. Somekh (eds), *The Sage Handbook of Educational Action Research*, London: Sage.

CCREC (Center for Collaborative Research for an Equitable California) (n.d.) <http://ccrec.ucsc.edu/research> [accessed 31 January 2013].

Chambers, R. (1992), 'Rural Appraisal: Rapid, Relaxed and Participatory', IDS Discussion Paper 311, Institute of Development Studies <http://opendocs.ids.ac.uk/opendocs/bitstream/handle/123456789/774/Dp311.pdf?sequence=1> [accessed 31 January 2013].

Chappell, A. (2000), 'The Emergence of Participatory Methodology in Learning Disability Research: Understanding the Context', *British Journal of Learning Disabilities*, 28(1): 38–43.

Charmaz, K. (2008), 'Views from the Margins: Voices, Silences and Suffering', *Qualitative Research in Psychology*, 5(1): 7–18.

Chevalier, J. M. and Buckles, D. J. (2013), *Participatory Action Research: Theory and Methods for Engaged Inquiry*, Abingdon: Routledge.

Cho, J. and Trent, A. (2006), 'Validity in Qualitative Research Revisited', *Qualitative Research*, 6: 319–40.

Clark, A. (2001), 'How to Listen to Very Young Children: The Mosaic Approach', *Child Care in Practice*, 7(4): 333–41.

— (2010), *Transforming Children's Spaces: Children's and Adults' Participation in Designing Learning Environments*, London: Routledge.

Clarke, G., Boorman, G. and Nind, M. (2011), '"If They Don't Listen I Shout, and When I Shout They Listen": Hearing the Voices of Girls With Behavioural, Emotional and Social Difficulties', *British Educational Research Journal*, 37(5): 765–80.

Cleaver, F. (1999), 'Paradoxes of Participation: Questioning Participatory Approaches to Development', *Journal of International Development*, 11: 597–612.

Clement, T. (2003), 'An Ethnography of People First Anytown', unpublished Ph.D. thesis, Milton Keynes: Open University.

Clough, P. and Barton, L. (1998), *Articulating with Difficulty: Research Voices in Inclusive Education*, London: Paul Chapman.

Coad, J. and Evans, R. (2008), 'Reflections on Practical Approaches to Involving Children and Young People in the Data Analysis Process', *Children and Society*, 22: 41–52.

Conolly, A. (2008), 'Challenges of Generating Qualitative Data with Socially Excluded Young People', *International Journal of Social Research Methodology*, 11(3): 201–14.

Cook, T. (2012), 'Where Participatory Approaches Meet Pragmatism in Funded (Health) Research: The Challenge of Finding Meaningful Spaces', *Forum Qualitative Sozialforschung/Forum: Qualitative Social Research*, 13(1), Art. 18 <http://nbn-resolving.de/urn:nbn:de:0114-fqs1201187>.

Cooke, B. and Kothari, U. (2001), 'The Case for Participation as Tyranny', in B. Cooke and U. Kothari (eds), *Participation: The New Tyranny?*, London: Zed Books.

Corbett, J. (1998), '"Voice" in Emancipatory Research: Imaginative Listening', in P. Clough and L. Barton (eds), *Articulating with Difficulty: Research Voices in Inclusive Education*, London: Paul Chapman.

Cornwall, A. (2008), 'Unpacking "Participation" Models, Meanings and Practices', *Community Development Journal*, 43(3): 269–83.

Cornwall, A. and Jewkes, R. (1995), 'What Is Participatory Research?' *Social Science and Medicine*, 41(12): 667–76.

Crow, G. (2010), 'Democratising Social Research', *Methods News*, Winter <http://eprints.ncrm.ac.uk/1594/1/MethodsNews_winter2010.pdf> [accessed 31 January 2013].

Danieli, A. and Woodhams, C. (2005), 'Emancipatory Research Methodology and Disability: A Critique', *International Journal of Social Research Methodology*, 8(4): 281–96.

Dockett, S. and Perry, B. (2011), 'Researching with Young Children: Seeking Assent', *Child Indicators Research*, 4: 231–47.

DuBois, B. (1983), 'Towards a Methodology for Feminist Research', in G. Bowles and R.Duelli Klein (eds), *Theories of Women's Studies*, London: Routledge and Kegan Paul.

Durham Community Research Team (2011), *Connected Communities--Community-based Participatory Research: Ethical Challenges* <www.ahrc.ac.uk/Funding-Opportunities/Research-funding/Connected-Communities/Scoping-studies-and-reviews/Documents/Community-based%20Participatory%20Research.pdf> [accessed 4 July 2013].

Edwards, R. and Alexander, C. (2011), 'Researching with Peer/Community Researchers', in M. Williams and W. P. Vogt (eds), *The Sage Handbook of Innovation in Social Science Research Methods*, London: Sage.

Elliot, J. (2009), 'Building Educational Theory through Action Research', in S. Noffke and B. Somekh (eds), *The Sage Handbook of Educational Action Research*, London: Sage.

Fals-Borda, O. (1991), 'Some Basic Ingredients', in O. Fals-Borda and M. Rahman (eds), *Action and Knowledge: Breaking the Monopoly with Participatory Action Research*, New York: Apex.

Fals-Borda, O. and Rahman, M. (eds) (1991), *Action and Knowledge: Breaking the Monopoly with Participatory Action Research*, New York: Apex.

Fenge, L. (2010), 'Striving towards Inclusive Research: An Example of Participatory Action Research with Older Lesbians and Gay Men', *British Journal of Social Work*, 40: 878–94.

Fergusson, A. (2012), 'Back to the Future: Moving Forward with Practitioner Research', in P. Jones, T. Whitehurst and J. Egerton (eds), *Creating Meaningful Inquiry in Inclusive Classrooms: Practitioners Stories of Research*, Abingdon: Routledge.

Fielding, M. (2004), 'Transformative Approaches to Student Voice: Theoretical Underpinnings, Recalcitrant Realities', *British Educational Research Journal*, 30(2): 295–311.

Fisher, K. R. and Robinson, S. (2010), 'Will Policy Makers Hear My Disability Experience? How Participatory Research Contributes to Managing Interest Conflict in Policy Implementation', *Social Policy and Society*, 9(2): 207–20.

Fisher, W. R. (1984), 'Narration as a Human Communication Paradigm', *Communication Monographs*, 51: 1–22.

Foucault, M. (1989), *The Order of Things: An Archaeology of the Human Sciences*, London: Routledge.

Frankham, J. (2009), *Partnership Research: A Review of Approaches and Challenges in Conducting Research in Partnership with Service Users,*

ESRC National Centre for Research Methods Review Paper 013 <http://eprints.ncrm.ac.uk/778/1/Frankham_May_09.pdf> [accessed 31 January 2013].

Freeman, M. and Mathison, S. (2009), *Researching Children's Experience*, New York: Guilford.

Freire, P. (1967), *Educação como Prática da Liberdade*, Rio de Janeiro: Paz e Terra.

— (1970), *Pedagogy of the Oppressed*, New York: Continuum.

French, S. and Swain, J. (1997), 'Changing Disability Research: Participating and Emancipatory Research with Disabled People', *Physiotherapy*, 83(1): 26–32.

Gallacher, L. and Gallagher, M. (2008), 'Methodological Immaturity in Childhood Research? Thinking through "Participatory Methods"', *Childhood*, 15(4): 499–516.

Goodley, D. (2000), *Self-Advocacy in the Lives of People with Learning Disabilities*, Buckingham: Open University Press.

Grant, G. (2013), 'Participatory Research – Some Thoughts on Paradigms and Partnerships', *Towards Equal and Active Citizenship: Pushing the Boundaries of Participatory Research with People with Learning Disabilities*, ESRC Seminar series, University of Plymouth, January.

Grant, G. and Ramcharan, P. (2007), *Valuing People and Research: The Learning Disability Research Initiative*, Overview Report, Department of Health.

Greene, S. (2009), *Accessing Children's Perspectives and Experience: Some Impediments*, Advancing Participatory Research Methods with Children and Young People. NCRM/Child Well-Being Research Centre. London, February.

Griffiths, M. (1998), *Educational Research for Social Justice: Getting Off the Fence*, Buckingham: Open University Press.

— (2009), 'Action Research for/as/Mindful of Social Justice', in S. Noffke and B. Somekh (eds), *The Sage Handbook of Educational Action Research*, London: Sage.

Grover, S. (2004), '"Why Won't They Listen to Us?" On Giving Power and Voice to Children Participating in Social Research', *Childhood*, 11(1): 81–93.

Hammersley, M. (2013), *What is Qualitative Research?* London: Bloomsbury Academic.

Harding, S. (2004), *The Feminist Standpoint Theory Reader: Intellectual and Political Controversies*, New York: Routledge.

Haw, K. and Hadfield, M. (2011), *Video in Social Science Research: Functions and Forms*, Abingdon: Routledge.

Heron, J. (1996), *Cooperative Enquiry: Research into the Human Condition*, London: Sage.

High, C. (2010), *What is Participatory Video?* [online video], Oxford: Fourth Research Methods Festival <www.ncrm.ac.uk/TandE/video/RMF2010/pages/29_ParticipateVid.php> [accessed 11 February 2013].

Holland, S., Renold, E., Ross, N. and Hillman, A. (2008), *Rights, 'Right On' Or The Right Thing to Do? A Critical Exploration of Young People's Engagement in Participative Social Work Research*, NCRM Working Paper Series 07/08 <http://eprints.ncrm.ac.uk/460/1/0708%2520critical%2520exploration.pdf> [accessed 31 January 2013].

hooks, b. (1990), *Yearning: Race, Gender and Politics*, Boston, MA: South End Press.

International Collaboration for Participatory Health Research (ICPHR) (2013), *Position Paper 1: What Is Participatory Health Research?* Version: Mai 2013. Berlin: International Collaboration for Participatory Health Research.

Johnson, K. (2009), 'No Longer Researching About Us Without Us: A Researcher's Reflection on Rights and Inclusive Research in Ireland', *British Journal of Learning Disabilities*, 37: 250–6.

Jones, P., Whitehurst, T. and Hawley, K. (2012), 'Reclaiming Research: Connecting Research to Practitioners', in P. Jones, T. Whitehurst and J. Egerton (eds), *Creating Meaningful Inquiry in Inclusive Classrooms: Practitioners' Stories of Research*, Abingdon: Routledge.

Kellett, M. (2005a), *Children as Active Researchers: A New Research Paradigm for the 21st Century?* NCRM Methods Review Paper/003 <http://eprints.ncrm.ac.uk/87/1/MethodsReviewPaperNCRM-003.pdf> [accessed 31 January 2013].

— (2005b), *How to Develop Children as Researchers*, London: Sage.

— (2011), 'Empowering Children and Young People as Researchers: Overcoming Barriers and Building Capacity', *Child Indicators Research*, 4: 205–19.

Kellett, M., Forrest, R., Dent, N. and Ward, S. (2004), '"Just Teach Us the Skills Please, We'll Do the Rest": Empowering Ten-Year-Olds as Active Researchers', *Children and Society*, 18(5): 329–43.

Kellett, M., with original research contributions by young people with a learning disability: Allan Aoslin, Ross Baines, Alice Clancy,

Lizzie Jewiss-Hayden, Ryan Singh and Josh Strudgwick (2010), 'WeCan2: Exploring the Implications of Young People with Learning Disabilities Engaging in Their Own Research', *European Journal of Special Needs Education*, 25(1): 31–44.

Kesby, M. (2000), 'Participatory Diagramming: Deploying Qualitative Methods through an Action Research Methodology', *Area*, 32(4): 423–35.

— (2007), 'Spatialising Participatory Approaches: The Contribution of Geography to a Mature Debate', *Environment and Planning*, 39(12): 2813–31.

Kiernan, C. (1999), 'Participation in Research by People with Learning Disabilities: Origins and Issues', *British Journal of Learning Disabilities*, 27(2): 43–7.

Kitchen, R. (2000), 'The Researched Opinions on Research: Disabled People and Disability Research', *Disability and Society*, 15: 25–47.

Lassiter, E. (2005), 'Collaborative Ethnography and Public Anthropology', *Current Anthropology*, 46(1): 83–106.

Lather, P. (1986), 'Research as Praxis', *Harvard Educational Review*, 56(3): 257–77.

— (1991), *Getting Smart: Feminist Research and Pedagogy With/in the Postmodern*, New York/London: Routledge.

Leitch, R., Gardner, J., Mitchell, S., Lundy, L., Odena, O., Galanouli, D., et al. (2007), 'Consulting Pupils in Assessment for Learning Classrooms: The Twists and Turns of Working with Students as Co-Researchers', *Educational Action Research*, 15(3): 459–78.

Lewis, A., Parsons, S. and Robertson, C. (2007), *My School, My Family, My Life: Telling It Like It Is. A Study Drawing on the Experiences of Disabled Children, Young People and Their Families in Great Britain in 2006*, London: Disability Rights Commission/Birmingham: University of Birmingham, School of Education <http://83.137.212.42/sitearchive/DRC/library/research> [accessed 31 January 2013].

Lewis, A., Parsons, S., Robertson, C., Feiler, A., Tarleton, B., Watson, D., et al. (2008), 'Reference, or Advisory, Groups Involving Disabled People: Reflections from Three Contrasting Research Projects', *British Journal of Special Education*, 35(2): 78–84.

Lindlow, V. (1996), *User Involvement: Community Service Users as Consultants and Trainers*, Leeds, West Yorkshire: Department of Health, National Health Service Executive Community Care Branch.

Lykes, B. (1989), 'Dialogue with Guatamalan Indian Women: Critical Perspectives on Constructing Collaborative Research', in R. K. Unger (ed.), *Representations: Social Constructions of Gender*, Amityville, NY: Baywood.

McClelland, S. I. and Fine, M. (2008), 'Writing on Cellophane', in K. Gallagher (ed.), *The Methodological Dilemma. Creative, Critical and Collaborative Approaches to Research*, Abingdon: Routledge.

McClimens, A. (2008), 'This Is My Truth, Tell Me Yours: Exploring the Internal Tensions with Collaborative Learning Disability Research', *British Journal of Learning Disabilities*, 36(4): 271–6.

McLaren, P. L. and Giarelli, J. M. (1995), 'Introduction: Critical Theory and Educational Research', in P. L. McLaren and J. M. Giarelli (eds), *Critical Theory and Educational Research*, Albany, NY: State University of New York Press.

McLarty, M. M. and Gibson, J. W. (2000), 'Using Video Technology in Emancipatory Research', *European Journal of Special Needs Education*, 15(2): 38–48.

MacLeod, A., Lewis, A. and Robertson, C. (2013), ' "CHARLIE: PLEASE RESPOND!" Using a Participatory Methodology with Individuals on the Autism Spectrum', *International Journal of Research and Method in Education*, doi.org/10.1080/1743727X.2013.776528

McTaggart, R. (1997), 'Guiding Principles for Participatory Action Research', in R. McTaggart (ed.), *Participatory Action Research: International contexts and consequences*, Albany, NY: State University of New York Press.

Mason, J. and Danby, S. (2011), 'Children as Experts in Their Lives', *Child Indicators Research*, 4: 185–9.

Mercer, G. (2002), 'Emancipatory Disability Research', in C. Barnes, M. Oliver and L. Barton (eds), *Disability Studies Today*, Cambridge: Polity.

Milewa, T., Valentine, J. and Calman, M. (1999), 'Community Participation and Citizenship in British Health Care Planning: Narratives of Power and Involvement in the Changing Welfare State', *Sociology of Health and Illness*, 21(4): 445–65.

Minkler, M. (2005), 'Community-Based Research Partnerships: Challenges and Opportunities', *Journal of Urban Health*, 82(2) (supplement 2): 3–12.

Minkler, M. and Wallerstein, N. (2008), 'Introduction to CBPR: New Issues and Emphases', in M. Minkler and N. Wallerstein (eds),

Community-Based Participatory Research for Health: From Process to Outcomes, 2nd edn, San Francisco: Wiley.

Moore, R. and Muller, J. (1999), 'The Discourse of "Voice" and the Problem of Knowledge and Identity in the Sociology of Education', *British Journal of Sociology of Education*, 20(2): 89–206.

Narayanasamy, N. (2009), *Participatory Rural Appraisal: Principles, Methods, and Application*, London: Sage.

Newman, J. (2002), 'Changing Governance, Changing Equality? New Labour, Modernisation and Public Services', *Public Money and Management*, January–March, 7–13.

Nind, M. (2011), 'Participatory Data Analysis: A step Too Far?' *Qualitative Research*, 11(4): 349–63.

Nind, M. and Vinha, H. (2012), *Doing Research Inclusively, Doing Research Well? Report of the Study: Quality and Capacity in Inclusive Research with People with Learning Disabilities.* Research report, University of Southampton <www.southampton.ac.uk/education/research/projects/quality_and_capacity_in_inclusive_research_with_learning_disabilities.page> [accessed 31 January 2013].

— (2013), 'Doing Research Inclusively: Bridges to Multiple Possibilities in Inclusive Research', *British Journal of Learning Disabilities*, i1–8, Early View, doi:10.1111/bld.12013.

Nind, M., Wiles, R. A., Bengry-Howell, A. and Crow, G. P. (2012), 'Methodological Innovation and Research Ethics: Forces in Tension or Forces in Harmony?' *Qualitative Research*, i1–12, Online First, doi:10.1177/1468794112455042.

Noffke, S. (2009), 'Revisiting the Professional, Personal, and Political Dimensions of Action Research', in S. Noffke and B. Somekh (eds), *The Sage Handbook of Educational Action Research*, London: Sage.

Oliver, M. (1992), 'Changing the Social Relations of Research Production', *Disability, Handicap and Society*, 7(2): 1–15.

— (1997), 'Emancipatory Research: Realistic Goal or Impossible Dream?' in C.Barnes and G.Mercer (eds), *Doing Disability Research*, Leeds: Disability Press.

Pain, R., Whitman, G., Milledge, D. and Lune Rivers Trust (n.d.), *Participatory Action Research Toolkit: An Introduction to Using PAR as an Approach to Learning, Research and Action* <www.dur.ac.uk/resources/beacon/PARtoolkit.pdf> [accessed 31 January 2013].

Porter, G., Townsend, J. and Hampshire, K. (2012), 'Children and Young People as Producers of Knowledge', *Children's Geographies*, 10(2): 31–4.

Punch, S. (2002), 'Research with Children. The Same or Different from Research with Adults?' *Childhood*, 9(3): 321–41.

Rahman, M. A. (1991), 'The Theoretical Standpoint of PAR', in O. Fals-Borda and M. Rahman (eds), *Action and Knowledge. Breaking the Monopoly with Participatory Action Research*, New York: Apex.

Reason, P. (ed.) (1988), *Human Inquiry in Action: Developments in New Paradigm Research*, London: Sage.

Reason, P. and Bradbury, H. (eds) (2008), *Handbook of Action Research*, 2nd edn, London/Thousand Oaks: Sage.

Reinharz, S. (1983), 'Experiential Analysis: A Contribution to Feminist Research', in G. Bowles and R.Duelli Klein (eds), *Theories of Women's Studies*, London: Routledge and Kegan Paul.

— (1992), *Feminist Methods in Social Research*, Oxford: Oxford University Press.

Ross, F., Donovan S., Brearley S., Victor C., Cottee M., Crowther P., et al. (2005), 'Involving Older People in Research: Methodological Issues', *Health and Social Care in the Community*, 13(3): 268–75.

Schneider, B. (2010), *Hearing (Our) Voices: Participatory Research in Mental Health*, Toronto: University of Toronto Press.

Shakespeare, T. (1996), 'Rules of Engagement: Doing Disability Research', *Disability and Society*, 11(1): 15–19.

Sherwood, G. (2011), 'Exploring Parents' Experiences of Support When They Have a Young Child with a Learning Disability', Ph.D. thesis, University of Southampton.

Sin, C. H. and Fong, J. (2010), 'Commissioning Research, Promoting Equality: Reflections on the Disability Rights Commission's Experiences of Involving Disabled Children and Young People', *Children's Geographies*, 8(1): 9–24.

Smith, L. Tuhiwai (2012), *Decolonizing Methodologies: Research and Indigenous Peoples*, 2nd edn, London: Zed Books.

Springett, J., Wright, M. T. and Roche, B. (2011), *Developing Quality Criteria for Participatory Health Research. Discussion Paper SP I 2011-302*, April 2011 <www.wzb.eu/de/forschung/bildung-arbeit-und-lebenschancen/public-health> [accessed 4 July 2013].

Staddon, P. (2012), 'No Blame, No Shame: Towards a Social Model of Alcohol Dependency – A Story from Emancipatory Research', in P. Beresford and S. Carr (eds), *Social Care, Service Users and User Involvement*, London: Jessica Kingsley.

Staley, K. (2009), Public Involvement in NHS, Public Health and Social
    Care Research. Involve <www.invo.org.uk/wpcontent/uploads/2011/11/
    Involve_Exploring_Impactfinal28.10.09.pdf> [accessed 2 July 2013].

Sumara, D. J. and Luce-Kapler, R. (1993), 'Action Research as a Writerly
    Text: Locating Colabouring in Collaboration', *Educational Action
    Research*, 1(3): 387–96.

Thomas, N. and O'Kane, C. (1998), 'The Ethics of Participatory Research
    with Children', *Children and Society*, 12: 336–48.

Thomson, F. (2007), 'Are Methodologies for Children Keeping Them in
    Their Place?' *Children's Geographies*, 5(3): 207–18.

Thomson, P. and Gunter, H. (2006), 'From "Consulting Pupils" to "Pupils as
    Researchers": A Situated Case Narrative', *British Educational Research
    Journal*, 32(6): 839–56.

Thorne, B. (2002), 'From Silence into Voice: Bringing Children More Fully
    into Knowledge', *Childhood*, 9(3): 251–4.

Todd, L. (2012), Critical Dialogue, Critical Methodologies: Bridging the
    Research Gap to Young People's Participation in Evaluating Children's
    Services', *Children's Geographies*, 10(2): 87–200.

Torre, M. E. (2005), 'The Alchemy of Integrated Spaces: Youth
    Participation in Research Collectives of Difference', in L. Weis and
    M. Fine (eds), *Beyond Silenced Voices*, 2nd edn, Albany, NY: State
    University of New York Press.

Torre, M. E. and Fine, M. (2006), 'Participatory Action Research (PAR)
    by Youth', in L. Sherrod (ed.), *Youth Activism: An International
    Encyclopedia*, Westport, CT: Greenwood.

Torre, M. E., Fine, M., Boudin, K., Bowen, I., Clark, J., Hylton, D., et al. (2001),
    'A Space for Co-Constructing Counter Stories under Surveillance',
    International Journal of Critical Psychology, 4: 49–166.

Townson, L., Macauley, S., Harkness, E., Chapman, R., Docherty, A., Dias,
    J., et al. (2004), 'We Are All in the Same Boat: Doing "People-Led
    Research"', *British Journal of Learning Disabilities*, 32: 72–6.

United Nations (1989), *Convention on the Rights of the Child*, Geneva:
    United Nations.

— (2006), *Convention on the Rights of Persons with Disabilities*, New York:
    United Nations.

Van Blerk, L. and Ansell, N. (2007), 'Participatory Feedback and
    Dissemination with and for Children: Reflections from Research with

Young Migrants in Southern Africa', *Children's Geographies*, 5(3): 313–24.

Vinha, M. H. G. L. (2011), 'Learners' Perspectives of Identity and Difference: A Narrative Study on Visual and Verbal Representation of Self and Other', Ph.D. thesis, University of Southampton.

Wallerstein, N. and Duran, B. (2008), 'The Theoretical, Historical and Practical Roots of CBPR', in M. Minkler and N. Wallerstein (eds), *Community-Based Participatory Research for Health: From Process to Outcomes*, 2nd edn, San Francisco: Wiley.

Walmsley, J. (2004), 'Inclusive Learning Disability Research: The (Nondisabled) Researcher's Role', *British Journal of Learning Disabilities*, 32: 65–71.

Walmsley, J. and Johnson, K. (2003), *Inclusive Research with People with Learning Disabilities: Past, Present and Futures*, London: Jessica Kingsley.

Walmsley, J. with CEPF (in press), 'Telling the History of Self Advocacy: A Challenge for Inclusive Research', *Journal of Applied Research in Intellectual Disability*.

Warren, L. and Boxall, K. (2009), 'Service Users In and Out of the Academy: Collusion in Exclusion?' *Social Work Education*, 28(3): 281–97.

Watson, D., Tarleton, B. and Feiler, A. (2007), *I Want to Choose Too: A Resource Pack for Teachers and Other Professionals*, Norah Fry Research Centre <www.bris.ac.uk/norahfry> [accessed 1 January 2013].

Wenger, E. (1998), *Communities of Practice: Learning, Meaning and Identity*, New York: Cambridge University Press.

White, S. A. (2003), *Participatory Video: Images That Transform and Empower*, Thousand Oaks, CA: Sage.

Whitmore, E. and McGee, C. (2001), 'Six Street Youth Who Could . . .', in P. Reason and H. Bradbury (eds), *Handbook of Action Research*, London/Thousand Oaks, CA: Sage.

Winter, R. (1998), 'Finding a Voice—Thinking with Others: A Conception of Action Research', *Educational Action Research*, 6(1): 53–68.

Wright, M. T., Roche, B., von Unger, H., Block, M. and Gardner, B. (2010), 'A Call for an International Collaboration on Participatory Research for Health', *Health Promotion International*, 25(1): 115–22.

Yardley, A. C. (2011), 'Children as Experts in Their Own Lives: Reflections on the Principles of Creative Collaboration', *Child Indicators Research*, 4: 191–204.

Zarb, G. (1992), 'On the Road to Damascus: First Steps towards Changing the Relations of Research Production', *Disability, Handicap and Society,* 7(2): 125–38.

Zeni, J. (2009), 'Ethics and the "Personal" in Action Research', in S. Noffke and B. Somekh (eds), *The Sage Handbook of Educational Action Research,* London: Sage.

Index

Page numbers in **bold** refer to figures/tables.

9 781350 188761